Lady Annabel Goldsmith is a daughter of the 8th Marquess of Londonderry. Her name is indelibly associated with the London nightclub Annabel's, whose founder, Mark Birley, she married at the age of nineteen, and with whom she had three children. In 1978 she married James Goldsmith and had three more children. She is also the author of *Annabel: An Unconventional Life* and *Copper: A Dog's Life*.

No Invitation Required

THE PELHAM COTTAGE YEARS

Annabel Goldsmith

PHOENIX

A PHOENIX PAPERBACK

First published in Great Britain in 2009
by Weidenfeld & Nicolson
This paperback edition published in 2010
by Phoenix,
an imprint of Orion Books Ltd,
Orion House, 5 Upper St Martin's Lane,
London WC2H 9EA

An Hachette UK company

1 3 5 7 9 10 8 6 4 2

A CIP catalogue record for this book
is available from the British Library.

ISBN 978-0-7538-2338-5

Printed and bound in Great Britain by
CPI Mackays, Chatham, Kent

The Orion Publishing Group's policy is to use papers that
are natural, renewable and recyclable products and
made from wood grown in sustainable forests. The logging
and manufacturing processes are expected to conform to
the environmental regulations of the country of origin.

www.orionbooks.co.uk

To Mark and Rupert

CONTENTS

LIST OF ILLUSTRATIONS

Wynyard Hall

My grandmother Edith in her Women's Legion
    uniform

Mark and me on our wedding day

Mark with his dog, Help

Mark in the South of France

Mrs White on her ninetieth birthday

John Aspinall ('Aspers') and Teddy with two of his
    gorillas

Aspers and Teddy with one of the tigers

Aspers with one of his elephants

Aspers giving a rhino a piece of chocolate

Aspers with John Huston

Patrick Plunket at Pelham Cottage

Patrick at The Mount

Geoffrey Keating

Geoffrey and his daughter, Rima

Claus von Bülow
Sunny von Bülow and Cosima
Claus and Cosima
Tony Lambton in Tuscany
Tony at Pelham Cottage
David Frost and the Shah of Persia
David, Carina and their three sons
David and Carina at Ormeley Lodge
Rupert, Mark and me, with Noodle
India Jane and me
Rupert having his hand stitched
My favourite photograph of Rupert
Rupert in St Anton

PREFACE

The night before I left Pelham Cottage, I had a feeling of overwhelming sadness. I might have been moving to Australia instead of to my new home, Ormeley Lodge, which lies between Richmond Park and Ham Common. I could not imagine finding the same warm cosiness and feeling of safety that I experienced at Pelham Cottage. I had lived there for so many years and throughout the good times and occasional bad times, I truly loved it.

In this book I have written about eleven characters who stood out during those years, but there were so many more of my close friends who were part of my life there. It would have been impossible to write about them all without the book becoming the length of the Bible. Amongst many others, there were Simon and Annabel Elliot, Mark and Liz Brocklehurst, my sister Jane and later her husband Max Rayne, my brother Alastair Londonderry and his wife Nico (my best and closest friend), Gill Goldsmith (my fellow sun-worshipper, who spent hours sunbathing on the terrace and cooling off in the children's paddling pool). One of the most frequent visitors was Elizabeth of Yugoslavia, along with her three children, Catherine, Tina and Nicholas, the youngest, affectionately known as 'the Toad'. And then there were the children, not only mine, but all their friends. The garden at times reminded me of Oscar Wilde's enchanting story *The Selfish Giant*, whose garden was alive with children.

The first morning I awoke at Ormeley, I realised that I had not completely left Pelham Cottage. Instead, I had brought it with me as most of the furniture was in my bedroom. Since it was almost the length of Pelham Cottage, most of the furniture I had lived with fitted into it, including the drawing-room sofa, which had so often been used as a bed for those who came to lunch and stayed.

Over the next few years, Pelham Cottage was sold and re-sold and finally ended up as it had been many years before, as one house: Park House. There is no longer any Pelham Cottage and I have never been able to bring myself to go back.

CHAPTER ONE

PELHAM COTTAGE

The day I discovered Pelham Cottage was a day that both changed and enhanced my entire life.

In 1958 I was twenty-three years old, and my husband Mark and I were living in a small terraced house in Halsey Street in Chelsea. Rupert was two and I had just given birth to my second son Robin. It was clearly time for a move, but as yet I had had no luck finding anywhere suitable. I was determined yet despondent, and had called on my close friends to keep an eye out for something Mark and I might like. One evening, I picked up the phone to hear my friend Maria Harrison's excitedly urgent voice, her wonderful Latvian accent even more pronounced than usual: 'Darling! I have heard of an amazing little house somewhere off Pelham Street in Kensington. You absolutely must go and look at it, first thing in the morning.' There was such conviction and energy in her voice and I had for so long trusted her exquisite taste in just about everything that early the next morning I set off to look for this mysterious house in Pelham Street.

I wandered up and down looking for anything that might possibly be Pelham Cottage, then spotted a little lane running off the street. At the bottom on the right was a rather dilapidated black gate with the words 'Pelham Cottage' written on it. I was transfixed by these words, and driven forward by a determination to see what lay beyond. I looked up to assess whether I could climb over – for I assumed the gate must be locked – but in that instant, something made me stop and turn the little handle. To my surprise it opened, and I stepped inside.

I had the same sensation I am sure Mary Lennox must have had when she discovered the secret garden in Frances Hodgson Burnett's book, and I can still remember the catch of pure excitement in my throat. I stood for a moment and, like Mary, listened to the stillness. I could not believe that such an oasis could exist only a few yards from South Kensington Tube station. In my daze of delight, I knew immediately that I had stumbled upon something magical here, and before I knew what I was doing I was racing up the road to find a phone box to call Mark. Breathlessly, I told him that I had found the house of our dreams and that he had to come *right away*. Fifteen minutes later, having excused himself from a meeting at his office at J. Walter Thompson, he was standing beside me in the garden. I could see from his expression, from the way he was taking it all in, that he too had fallen instantly in love with the place.

Together we explored the large garden somewhat silently and reverentially, and when we came up to the back of the house we tried our luck with the back door. However, it was locked and we were unable to get inside. It was a two-storey Regency building, painted white, and looking through the windows we could see that it was empty and quiet and uncluttered. I could tell that it wasn't much larger than our current home, but this suddenly did not seem to matter to me. As we stood together under one of the huge lime trees, facing the garden, I said slowly: 'We've found our home. We just have to live here. I can feel it physically, from deep down inside of me.' His response was more cautious – he agreed it was a dream house but, ever the practical man, he needed to know if we could build on to the side of it to make it bigger. But he absolutely agreed we should make an offer.

Back in Chelsea I called Maria and, trembling with excitement, told her: 'I found it, and the gate was open and I walked in and I just *knew*. I made Mark come straight away and we're going to try and buy it.' She of course was delighted – as my surrogate mother, she always wanted what was best for me. As soon as I put the phone down I set about haggling with my trustees, on whom I was dependent, and within a few frantic weeks managed to buy Pelham Cottage. And so it was on a glorious autumn day in 1959 that Mark and I, Rupert, Robin and my dog Noodle moved in. Almost immediately we began turning the cottage into the little gem that it became and remained for twenty years.

Here we were in this lovely clean, light shell – the floors throughout were wooden and the walls painted a bright white. There had not been anyone living in the house for some time, and so from the outset I felt very much as if we were able to establish our own personalities at Pelham Cottage. The study downstairs had large built-in bookcases – perfect for all our books – but we would need a great deal more furniture to fill up the drawing-room. The kitchen was just big enough for a table at which we could all eat, leaving the tiny dining-room for entertaining guests. There was a modest staff room downstairs too. Upstairs was also very small, only three bedrooms and two bathrooms, and so we found ourselves, as ever, cramped. Mark, with his enviable ability to turn little rooms into excit-ing, wondrous spaces, saw huge potential within the house, and he set about commissioning the famous architect Philip Jebb to build an extension on the side of the house. This eventually accommodated a nursery with a balcony (upon which, ever the sun-worshipper,

I would spend endless happy hours sitting talking with friends and giving the children their meals) and Mark's ship's cabin in which he installed mahogany cupboards for his legendary collection of suits and shoes.

As the house settled around us and we settled into it, I felt an intense happiness: Pelham Cottage was my nest, a safe haven to which I could always return with great comfort and inner peace. At this time in my life I was rather shy and lacking in confidence, not always able to cope with the endless dinners and parties that Mark so enjoyed going to. However, from the first night in Pelham Cottage to the day I left, whatever was happening around me, whatever turmoil I felt myself to be in, the house and the garden enclosed me and kept me safe within myself. They absorbed me from the outset.

Pelham Cottage appeared to be the front half of the adjoining building, Park House, and I was eager to discover the history of the place. Park House had been built in the mid-nineteenth century, when Kensington was still a village, by John Bonnin, a grocer turned developer. He built two cottages to the west side of Pelham Street (the lane I mentioned earlier) and was living in the northerly one – Pelham Cottage – in 1841. The other, Park Cottage, now Park House, was named after its first inhabitant Thomas Park, a local tailor. At the time we moved in, the houses were pleasing to look at – long and narrow, but treated in a pleasantly vernacular manner with informally planned interiors. There was a true beauty in the windows – in their shape and in the amount of light they let in and reflected throughout the house – a quality I have never really seen since. Approached only by narrow passageways from Pelham Street or Onslow Square, both cottages enjoy almost total exclusion and have been much sought after in recent years. Perhaps inevitably, over time, they have undergone substantial alteration. When, some years later, the decision was taken to build a large block of flats in part of the garden at the back of the adjoining 'orchard' that did not belong to the house, I made several protests, at one point climbing a tree the developers wanted to cut down. I refused to come down until they agreed to leave a few of the trees in the orchard; I felt very proud and feisty, having achieved this compromise.

The garden was of course an intrinsic part of the house, surrounding it entirely, and while the house was small, the garden was unusually large. This was because next to the property was a neglected bombsite where over the years bushes and trees had grown up, giving the extraordinary impression of a little orchard there in the very heart of Kensington.

The garden was a marvellous wilderness and we wondered what to do with it. We were so fortunate that when we moved in our neighbour at Park House was Lanning Roper – the most famous landscape gardener of the time – and in the early days he gave us advice on what to do with the garden. We didn't have enough money then, or the addiction to gardening that was necessary to be truly committed to changing it, but walking around the garden with Lanning and listening to him talk about the possibilities, I was aware of being in the presence of a visionary, marvelling at the way he could see things; and because, actually, as I later discovered, the gardening gene did lie within me, I was able to conjure up his words and ideas and dreams in my mind. I remember coming downstairs bleary-eyed one Sunday morning a few months after we moved in, and while waiting for the kettle to boil, catching sight of someone in the garden. On closer inspection I saw it was Lanning, who had sneaked in to plant some bulbs before we got up! He didn't see me watching him and I still laugh at the furtiveness of his mission. The bulbs flowered beautifully the next spring and I treated them with great care and gratitude.

I loved the garden's wildness, and for some years left it in its glorious natural state. However, I discovered that my view of it was not shared by some visitors we welcomed in when, early one summer, I rather stupidly agreed to open the garden for the National Gardens Scheme. At around 2 p.m. one day, ten very eager, bustling women arrived and I invited them to stroll around the garden. They looked at the few hastily bedded begonias and the plentiful supply of nettles and muttered to themselves, clearly disappointed. Recalling the advice of my painter friend Adrian Daintry, 'You could always take the visitors inside and show them Mark's cabin and his impressive collection of suits and his hundreds of pairs of Cleverley shoes', I whisked them into the house. They crowded into the cabin and made a few disapproving noises, but there could be no doubt they were still unsatisfied, so I took them hastily into the kitchen and served them my terrible lemon drizzle cake with icing that could break teeth. While their valiant attempts to eat it quietened them for a while, nothing could truly dispel their indignation and they left with the words 'Overflowing nettle beds, inedible sponge cake, shiny shoes – heavens!' ringing in my ears.

Soon after this humiliating experience Claire Ward, my great friend Tony Lambton's long-time companion, kindly took over and transformed our wilderness into a very pretty garden. She paved the area outside the French windows to the drawing-room, and planted hydrangeas and several varieties of roses to grow over the charming trellises that split the garden into two, one half taken up by a huge lawn and the other by a slightly more formal terrace. The end of the front lawn was flanked by the massive lime trees around which nothing could grow and which screened the view of the row of houses facing Pelham Cottage. I remember Claire and Reg White, my wonderful housekeeper's husband who tended the garden for us, having perpetual arguments about watering. He was anti-watering – 'You'll drown 'em' was his favourite phrase – and he and Claire would have polite but firm exchanges on its merits and demerits.

When I think back to my twenty years at Pelham Cottage, I am struck by the richness and variety of my life there – giving birth to three more children, India Jane, followed thirteen years later by Jemima, then Zac and welcoming Manes, Jimmy Goldsmith's son from his second marriage, and his other children, and experiencing other pleasurable (and turbulent) changes in my personal circumstances. Mark and I lived together there for some years before we separated, but even then he was still part of Pelham Cottage as he bought one of the properties in the lane nearby and was in and out much as before. When I began my affair with Jimmy in 1964, while being a big part of my life he rarely stayed at Pelham Cottage – I preferred to keep my life with Jimmy separate from the children when they were growing up.

So Pelham Cottage provided a haven, a sense of calm and belonging, that sustained me and shaped me fundamentally. However, it played a central role not only in *my* life: it struck me recently with a perfect clarity how significant Pelham Cottage was in the lives of all my friends and acquaintances who came to visit, and I look back on the vibrancy and variety of the ever-flowing stream of guests over the years with great fondness and pleasure. That first moment when I entered the garden through the unlocked black gate set a precedent. I too never locked it, so my family and friends could stroll in without prior warning or invitation, and for many years it was not unusual to return home from collecting the children from school to find several people sitting in the study or, if it was summer, in the sunny garden. I know that today I would find that sort of impromptu intrusion intolerable, but at that time I found it life-enhancing, and I welcomed the informality and perpetual surprise of who might be there to enrich and flavour my afternoon or evening.

Pelham Cottage, then, through the 1960s and 70s, became a sort of meeting point where people gathered to talk, drink, eat, sit in the garden and simply be among friends. Almost everyone who figures in this book recognised Pelham Cottage as somewhere different and special and loved spending time there. Our friend Claus von Bülow played backgammon with us most weekends; Mark's mother Rhoda would stay when she came to London, and I would invariably help her with hair-styling before an important evening party; my cousin Patrick Plunket loved it with a passion, and simply wandered in and out, usually at lunchtime; Geoffrey Keating, interesting and extraordinary himself, would bring the most interesting and extraordinary friends; the decorator Nicky Haslam, one of my closest friends, would wander round the drawing-room shifting furniture, then putting the room together again; my grandmother, Edith Marchioness of Londonderry, a formidable and highly respected gardener among many other talents, though not at all well at that time, loved the cottage and advised me on the garden.

And the children! I can still hear their laughter ringing through the years as they and their friends played in the garden. During term time the visiting friends were mostly India Jane's from St Paul's School, who were always welcome and added so much to the atmosphere. At the weekends Rupert and Robin would invite their friends to come, and the noise would be deafening as the boys chased the girls around the garden.

The garden was always alive with animals, especially after Robin won a guinea-pig at Battersea Fun Fair. Rover, as he was jokingly named, was carefully settled in a corner of the garden and became so tame that his hutch door was always left open. He would roam the garden accompanied by two large white rabbits which had been kindly donated – though much against my will – by a close friend. Then someone had the brilliant idea of giving India Jane a guinea-pig, supposedly a male, called Billy, who turned into Beatrice when hordes of little guinea-pigs were discovered a few weeks later. Over the next few months Beatrice and Rover and all their offspring became indiscriminately incestuous, and a whole tribe of guinea-pigs began to emerge. Occasionally I would be woken by cries of acute distress coming from the German maid living in one of the houses opposite. She would scream hysterically out of the window while dangling a furry object, Michael Jackson-style, that she had found in the bath or else-where, often brought in by one of their cats. In the end the guinea-pigs became too much for us – Rover, sadly, was killed by Geoffrey Keating's Jack Russell during one of their impromptu visits, Beatrice was spayed and several of the other guinea-pigs were found new homes. We ended up with four delightfully slow tortoises, one of whom lived to a ripe old age and moved with me from Pelham Cottage to Richmond.

Sadly, in the mid-1970s I realised that we had to move from Pelham Cottage – I had five children, Benjamin would appear in 1980 – and by this time Jimmy wanted us all to live together as one big family.

I had endless sleepless nights trying to think of some way we might remain at the house, but in the end it was impossible. When we found Ormeley Lodge on the edge of Richmond Park, I knew on one level that this would be an ideal home for us all, but the idea of leaving our present home terrified me and made me deeply unhappy. When we did make the move, I recreated Pelham Cottage in my bedroom, much to the mirth of my children. And in spite of my happiness at Ormeley, I still think of Pelham Cottage with love and nostalgia for the happy years my family, friends and I enjoyed there. Since we left it has changed hands many times and finally it was joined to Park House, making it one large house and one huge garden, and as such has become unrecognisable to me from both the outside and within.

And so, apart from deep inside my happiest thoughts, I have never been back there.

CHAPTER TWO

MARK BIRLEY

The day before Mark's funeral on 18 September 2007, India Jane and I went to St Paul's Church in Knightsbridge where the charming vicar, the Reverend Alan Gyle, was waiting for us. We had come to receive the coffin. On our way into the church I had spotted what looked like an abandoned trolley from Sainsbury's parked at the foot of the steps. The head undertaker, already sporting his top-hat, approached me with what must have been his permanently solemn face.

'I'm afraid, Lady Annabel, that the floral tributes on top of the coffin have made it too heavy for my men to carry,' he said apologetically. 'And this means we will have to bring the coffin in and out on a trolley.' Although I knew Mark would have been highly amused at this suggestion, there was no way I was going to agree to him being trolleyed in and out of his own funeral service; it would be too undignified, so a solution had to be found.

When I arrived at the church the next day I was deeply touched to see that the many 'floral tributes' had been arranged on the ground around the coffin, while the small bunch of white roses, the last of the summer blooms that I had picked from my garden at Ormeley the previous day, lay alone on top of it with a little note from the children and me.

I had made a vow with the children that we would try not to cry, and although the service was astonishingly moving we managed for most of the hour to keep our promises to one another. I had chosen his favourite hymns, among them 'Jerusalem' and 'I Vow to Thee, My Country'. 'The Londonderry Air' was played, the choir sang 'Ave Maria' quite beautifully and there were readings by friends and family, including one by me. After the moving but funny address by Peter Blond, Mark's oldest friend since they messed together at Eton, the glorious solo of 'A Nightingale Sang in Berkeley Square' brought a nostalgic smile to the faces of the whole congregation. The church, decorated with a mass of roses – the flowers always chosen by Mark to fill the vases at his club Annabel's – was packed with his family, friends, lovers and admirers. Only at the end of the service did the children and I find it impossible to keep to our plan not to weep. As the bagpipes sounded out the first long heart-wrenchingly lovely note of 'Amazing Grace' and the coffin began its final journey down the aisle, the sight of Mark's two dogs Tara the Alsatian and George the black Labrador, held on their leads by Don his Scottish chauffeur, following their master, was too much for anybody to bear. The floodgates opened; along with most of the congregation I cried all the way down the aisle only to be met by a barrage of photographers outside, who captured all of us with tears rolling down our cheeks.

In a way, those final moments summed up Mark for me. There were so many facets to his character that would have been familiar to the hundreds of people in the church that day: his immaculate taste, his elegance, his humour, his loyalty, his perfectionism, his bad temper and his hospitality. But many people who thought they knew him were unaware of a whole side that was apparent to only a few.

Most friends, of course, knew about his affection for dogs. Anyone who has been to Annabel's or Mark's Club will remember that they are filled with paintings of dogs, some valuable, some just simply paintings that captured Mark's unerring eye and moved him. I gave him a picture which became one of his favourites and he hung it in the dining-room of Mark's Club; it depicted a dog, balancing on a raft, looking very concerned as two puppies struggle in the water below. On that sunny September day of Mark's funeral, however, it was the sight of the devotion of his two last dogs which reminded me how his relationship with his dogs revealed the most endearing and the sweetest side of the man whom I had known and loved for over fifty years.

Mark's passion for dogs began with our marriage. When we met there had been only one dog in his life, a mothy black poodle that belonged to his mother's fierce, dour Scottish housekeeper Girvie. But my sister's wedding present to us transformed Mark's life. Jane gave us a hopelessly unhousetrainable smooth-haired black-and-tan dachshund puppy. Noodle slept deep down between us in our bed and as we weren't intending to have any children at that stage we lavished our love on him, little knowing that within a year our firstborn, Rupert, would appear.

Mark was not by nature paternal, preferring to have had only one child rather than the three I imposed upon him. All his paternal instincts for young dependent creatures were concentrated on dogs. We both treated Noodle, a highly intelligent animal with an unerring instinct for the geography of London, like a child, and I said to Mark one day when a row between us was getting very heated: 'Please don't swear in front of Noodle.'

When we lived in Halsey Street during 1954–8 Mrs Godfrey, a nice German lady who was a great friend of our alcoholic cook Frieda, used to come and help us out at dinner parties. Mr Godfrey, whom we rarely saw, was a rather bad-tempered and intimidating milkman with one leg. As a thank-you present for all her hard work I gave Mrs Godfrey a dachshund bitch called Mitzi with whom Noodle was more than a little in love. When we moved to Pelham Cottage, Noodle easily found his way down Pelham Street, across to Sloane Avenue and up through the little maze of streets that led to Mrs Godfrey's front door and to the promise of ecstasy that lay behind it in the shape of Mitzi on heat. When Mr Godfrey discovered that Mitzi was pregnant with Noodle's puppies he came straight round to see Mark and threatened to break his legs should his dog die during the birth. Mitzi proceeded to give birth to three puppies which Mrs Godfrey, with great originality, named Jane, Alastair (my brother's name) and Annabel.

One summer in the early 1960s Mark and I rented a small holiday house in the South of France which we shared with Mark's friend Mark Brocklehurst and a host of guests who came and went throughout our stay. Both Marks used to go out clubbing, and one night very late when I was fast asleep Mark appeared in our bedroom carrying a tiny brown dachshund puppy that he had found in a nightclub, fallen in love with and persuaded the owner to sell to him on the spot. Waking up with a start to see a new small dog on my bed, I was initially furious and stormed off to the spare bedroom.

However, the next morning I crept back along the passage to find the puppy wrapped protectively around Mark's head; she growled when I came in and I instantly melted. Seeing my change of heart, Mark told me he had already named her Midge and fully intended to keep her. After Noodle, Midge became the second big canine love of Mark's life; he had found her, rescued her, and he adored her and she him. Immigration rules were very strict regarding pets but we found a co-operative French vet who gave Midge a mild sedative and an anti-rabies shot. We packed her into Mark's airline bag and after a heart-hammering journey to London, undetected by the customs officers, Midge began her new life in England.

She soon settled into Pelham Cottage, bonded with Noodle and became the centre of Mark's life. His love for her was so great that even when he came home from work and was greeted by Rupert and Robin all soft and ready for bed in their pyjamas, it was Midge that he would grab and make a big fuss of and sit on his lap. Many years later, after Mark and I were separated, we continued to live opposite each other, sharing Midge at the weekends.

Noodle and Midge eventually had a daughter called Minnie. Unfortunately she was completely rejected by Midge, who refused to feed her or pay any attention to her at all, but my vet found two amazing women who hand-reared her. Happily she survived and was able to come back to us after a month. She was small and comical-looking and Mark and I had a delicious time fantasising about what she got up to. She had a whole nefarious existence involving bank robbery, murder and Russian spies invented for her by Mark and me, and which would be discussed by us in conversations and in letters in as serious a tone as if it was all fact rather than fiction. It was a lovely, mad running joke that can only develop between two people who love and care for each other and share a common ground in their love for animals. I recently found a letter that Mark wrote to me from London one summer, just after he had launched Annabel's in 1963 and while we were still living together; I must have been abroad at the time:

I suppose you must have heard the news by now if the London papers reach you. Minnie was taken away by the Police for questioning at about 4.30 a.m. I was woken up by a lot of banging and noise and felt Minnie creeping down one of my legs – a second later three detectives with revolvers rushed into the room and turned the lights on. I tried to bluff it out but they weren't having any and Minnie was quickly handcuffed and dragged away. She let out a low moan and showed the whites of her eyes. I know she had committed a terrible crime, probably the worst ever, but I couldn't help feeling a pang as I saw her small face pressed to the window of the police car. Mr Battle is helping and we are going to get a really good lawyer. BUT three Policemen!

I wonder now whether Mark wrote me such letters with a subconscious intention of reflecting the special early relationship he knew I had with my father. At boarding school I used to receive marvellous letters from him all about our four Scotties and the Tail Waggers' Club he had invented for them, with detailed day-to-day accounts of what they got up to at home at Wynyard Hall in County Durham. I showed Mark these letters and he loved them. In a sense he had assumed the role of father to me; I was only nineteen when we married – Mark was five years older – and with the early death of my mother from cancer when I was seventeen and four years later that of my father Mark seemed to feel a need to protect me. He always signed his letters to me 'Dad', which I found very touching and reassuring.

In the early 1970s when Midge was terribly ill, lying on my bed looking quite pathetic, on a little drip, Mark came in to say goodbye on his way to New York. The sight of this small sick dog, the last one which, through

Noodle, linked us to the early years of our marriage, was almost too much for him to bear and he burst into tears. While Mark was in mid-flight Midge died and I dreaded making the phone call to tell him the news; I knew all he wanted to hear was that she was better. Even when I cried for nine hours without stopping after Robin was attacked by a tigress at John Aspinall's zoo in 1971, Mark did not weep; much as he minded, he was too angry with me for allowing Robin into the cage and too shocked to respond to this terrible accident with tears. But the death of Midge represented a severing of a particular link between us, and in that moment his heart was broken.

After Mark and I had separated amicably at the end of the 1960s, and he had moved into one of the houses opposite Pelham Cottage, he decided that he wanted a dog of his own; perhaps then, as at many other stages in his life, he found a real source of comfort in the companionship and faithful nature of a dog. On a visit to Battersea Dogs' Home he noticed a golden-brown-coloured animal, a mixture of God knows what parentage, a dog with golden eyes, who gave him his paw through the bars of the kennel. Crossing the room to look at the other inmates, Mark turned round to see that the golden dog had once again put out his paw and was following him with those riveting eyes. Mark knew that this was the one, and he named him Help.

This latest love was uncontrollable. With Help there was never any question of successfully imposing discipline. I was always made to take him for a walk and felt quite ridiculous as I tore around Kensington Gardens and Hyde Park, looking absurd and provoking an equal mixture of mirth and concern in hopeless pursuit of this large misfit, shouting, 'Help! Help! Help!'

The moment we got to the park he was off, and without missing a stride he would typically snatch the sandwiches out of the hand of some poor workman having his lunch – who would then yell at me, 'Oi, I've lost my lunch!' And I would say: 'I'm frightfully sorry. Can I go and buy you some more?', by which time Help was down by the Serpentine gobbling up the package, brown paper and all, even happier if there was a jam doughnut inside as well. 'Bit late now,' the man would mutter, shuffling back to work still hungry.

Help was so agile, with his long legs, that if he was in full pelt he never stopped to see what was in his way and frequently jumped straight over prams; I became used to nannies looking at me in fury, and, much as I loved him, I dreaded taking him out. He even chased horses and would run round and round driving both animal and rider mad and there was nothing I could do to stop him. Mark, though, would not listen to my complaints. Occasionally Help would go missing and there would be a desperate search for him, but we soon learned that he would make his way back to Victoria Coach Station and sit there till we turned up. We used to wonder whom or what he was looking for there. Despite his naughtiness I felt huge compassion for this abandoned dog and admired Mark in his devotion for him.

One day Mark appeared in my garden at Pelham Cottage carrying two of the most adorable puppies I have ever seen. They were not, however, destined to remain small for long; this time Mark had given his heart to a pair of St Bernards. They were called Williams and Williamine, a brother and sister. Realising that the English climate, let alone the London pavements, were not ideal for these two enchanting mountain dogs, Mark took them to his flat in St Anton in Austria where they became quite famous, often to be seen trotting around the village. As Mark could not find a suitable vet there, whenever one of the St Bernards became ill he would fly out his London vet, Mr Giles, who would spend all day drinking Mark's wine and his schnapps and then go home and send him a colossal bill, pleased at this cushy little holiday. Williams and Williamine remained in Austria for good, looked after by Mark's mountain guide Arthur.

Blitz, a Rhodesian ridgeback, was one of the most challenging dogs Mark ever had. Quite simply, if Blitz didn't like you he would bite you. Mark was incapable of accepting that any of his dogs were ever in the wrong, and when Blitz happened to bite a woman on her ear during one of their walks, Mark refused to blame Blitz. 'She must have antagonised him,' he said. 'Blitz wouldn't hurt a fly.'

Actually, some people were frightened to come to his house, but Mark's love even for what would now certainly qualify as a dangerous dog was unconditional.

By this time he had bought Thurloe Lodge in South Kensington and Blitz was joined by a rough-haired Jack Russell called Jack and an assortment of working spaniels, all found for him by his friend Hedley Millington, the distinguished breeder of working spaniels and gundog keeper based in Cornwall. Hedley also found Mark a beautiful Alsatian called Bella, who became another love of his life, but even Bella was not above giving people a little nip now and again, administered so surreptitiously that Mark never noticed (not that he would have believed it, even if he had). When Bella died rather suddenly Mark was grief-stricken.

Tara and George were his last two dogs. Every night George slept on Mark's bed on the Tempur mattress that guarantees no backache and costs a fortune, but Mark preferred to sleep in his reclining chair as George seemed happier on the Ritz of all mattresses; as always, dogs came first. Inscribed on a cushion in the house were the words, 'This house is maintained for the comfort and security of my dogs. If you cannot accept that then you cannot accept me – so go away.'

When Mark and I first fell in love I think we both envisaged an old age surrounded by dogs and laughter, but about four years ago Mark fractured his hip and spent a long time in the Wellington Hospital in North London. Although it was not allowed, Don his chauffeur used to try to smuggle George and Tara into his room to cheer him up – once or twice he even managed it, much to Mark's delight.

I was in Spain on a family holiday in August 2007 when I heard that Mark had suffered a massive stroke. India Jane rang me from the hospital to say that the doctor thought he would not live for more than a few hours but had reminded her that the last sense to go is the hearing. India Jane put her mobile phone on loudspeaker and held it to his ear. 'I love you more than anything, you silly old bugger,' I told him. 'I have always loved you and I will miss you dreadfully.' As I said these words Jane saw a change appear on his face, then suddenly he stopped breathing.

During that final illness both Tara and George had slept in Mark's room at home every night up until the very end; after his death they refused to go into his bedroom, their own grief as apparent as ours. I still miss Mark dreadfully because over the years, despite us going our separate ways, we remained incredibly close, and I loved the intimate little lunches and dinners during which Mark would tease me mercilessly and try to persuade me to take a glass of whatever lethal liquor he was drinking saying: 'There's nothing more boring than a woman who doesn't drink.'

CHAPTER THREE

MRS WHITE

Mrs White – or Wags, as she became known in our family – came into my life in 1954 when Mark and I were living in the tiny flat above his mother Rhoda's home in St John's Wood. We were very untidy, and because it wasn't our own home we decided that in order for complete chaos to be kept at bay we needed some help with the cleaning. Mrs Trindle, our daily from my childhood London home at 101 Park Street, found Wags for me. 'She's not much to look at, but you should see her house,' she beamed. 'It's so clean you could eat your dinner off the floor.' And how right she proved to be. Mrs White was a perfectionist in everything she did, a characteristic that made her sparkle in Mark's eyes, being a perfectionist himself.

I had no idea when I opened the door to this ferocious-looking woman that she would become one of the most important people in my life, someone I would love and cherish to her dying day almost fifty years later. At the time I was only nineteen, and she was in her mid-forties. As she stood there on the doorstep, I was rather startled by her strange-coloured hair (later she told me that she had tried to dye it but it hadn't quite worked), her large glasses and, most of all, her no-nonsense expression and turned-down mouth which made her look permanently cross. Actually, as I was soon to discover, this first impression was mistaken, for the real Kitty White had beautiful hair that later turned a vibrant white, and she had a soft side to her nature, showing kindness and utter devotion to me and my family. She became my true friend and confidante and I still miss her every day since she died.

Mrs White took the job on the spot, and from that day until her retirement she helped me run my household. As we spent more time together, we would share things with each other – she had suffered, she told me with no hint of self-pity, a difficult upbringing. She had never met her father, and her mother had bullied her throughout her life, even once hitting her hard over the head with a frying pan. Still, Mrs White was a most dutiful daughter and was devoted to her mother, who lived with her and her husband Reg. Every day without fail she went home to make her lunch, and to the last she made sure she was well cared for. I looked forward to Mrs White's stories of the war – her work in a factory and her vivid memories of the house next door being bombed; she talked to me of her marriage to Reg, about her daughter Joyce and, later, when Joyce and her family moved to Cornwall, her deepest wish that her twin grandchildren might live nearer to her. I loved sitting chatting with her and sometimes we would go out for a snack together or to the cinema in the afternoon – we both enjoyed films about families, particularly *The Family Way* with Hayley Mills – or we would have a cup of tea and she would update me on the goings-on in *Coronation Street* or *Emergency Ward 10*. She always had a comment or two on what 'those doctors were up to'. This was the 1960s.

It always made me smile hearing Mrs White talk about Reg and her sex life – or lack of it. Reg had been a brave sailor during the war but when I came to know him he must have been the most henpecked and frustrated husband in the world. Mrs White had a total aversion to sex, and poor Reg had not been allowed to have what she termed 'his way' for many years. She explained to me that her 'polyps' had put an end to their sex life, an activity which had in fact been doomed from the start. Although she would not have liked to admit it, she must have been aware that Mark and I slept together because not even Mrs White could persuade herself that my pregnancies were the result of an immaculate conception. However, she preferred to believe, and I did not disillusion her, that Mark like all men had to have 'his way'. She used to divide my girlfriends into categories, 'them that did and them that didn't', meaning those who were a bit flighty and those who were chaste. Of course, she invariably got it all wrong, little realising that 'them that didn't' did, and rather often at that.

But Mrs White was not always easy to be with: growing up with the harsh stigma of illegitimacy had, I believe, made her defensive and hardened to the outside world, and over the years the shifting mood of our day-to-day existence came to be signalled by one glance at her expression as she arrived in the morning for work. A rare smiley face meant a good day was ahead, one that would be filled with light-hearted banter, which I enjoyed enormously; Mrs White had a sense of humour next to none, unless it was directed against her. If, though – as she did more often than not – she arrived wearing her customary scowl my heart would sink, because that would entail hours of coaxing to get her back into a good mood. Sometimes a good gossip about someone else's problems or a bit of subtle flattery would do the trick, but if all this failed I would just disappear, and hope her mood would have improved on my return.

Mrs White loved nothing better than a good misfortune and she was the first to notice when I 'fell pregnant', as she observed with a sideways look in December 1954. 'Yes, I'm afraid you've fallen,' she told me, with an expression that was somewhere between a grimace and a grin as I languished in bed feeling too sick to get up. 'Oh dear!' she sighed with relish, and brought me a cup of strong tea and a plate of Rich Tea biscuits. And through the following months as I continued to balloon in a most alarming manner, Mrs White – by now nicknamed Wags – took an active interest in my pregnancy, muttering ominously about the terrible pain I was about to experience. When the long-predicted and gruesome moment arrived in August 1955, Wags escorted me into the nursing-home at 27 Welbeck Street. She assured me that I was having a boy and naturally she was right. Rupert was born after the hours of agonising pain that she had accurately predicted. Of course, she fell instantly in love with him, as she did with all my children, and she was there to help me as soon as I came home.

The attic in St John's Wood was just too small to house the three of us and so Mark set about finding us somewhere new to live. Rupert and I were dispatched to stay with my father at Wynyard and when I came back to London I was delighted to find that Mark, with his exquisite taste, had turned an ordinary little house in Halsey Street into a mini-paradise and it was ready for us to move in to. Mrs Ruddy, my father's housekeeper from 101 Park Street where I had lived as a child, whispered to me that Mark had taken so much trouble getting it ready for me that I must tell him how much I liked it. However, my genuine delight at Mark's surprise was not shared by Mrs White. Bristling with fury at the sight of Mrs Ruddy, someone I had known all my life, in the way she always bristled with anyone close to me, Wags announced that she would find the house 'far too much, what with my sick mother and all'. She bristled even more when she discovered that Mrs Ruddy along with the rest of the staff at 101 Park Street would be present at Rupert's christening, and it took a great deal of cajoling to get her to attend. Ten months of working for Mark and me in St John's Wood had given her a sense of ownership, and she hated the thought of anyone else working for me as well.

Later, the move to Pelham Cottage was preceded by the usual days of grumbling from Mrs White, but having made the move, she soon became the doyenne of the house. In her heart she must have preferred it to no. 9 Halsey Street because it was on only two floors, hence no complaints about her varicose veins. She, like everyone else, loved Pelham Cottage, though once we got going with all the internal building work she moaned about the mess and the constant presence of the builders. She also built up an ongoing and lengthy feud with my first three children's nanny, Wendy

Jacob – it was never malicious and often hysterically funny – and they both adored the children.

Mrs White and Reg would arrange their summer holiday at Butlin's to coincide with our visit to our rented holiday home in Middleton-on-Sea in West Sussex, and they would come and spend time with us there. When we went abroad and couldn't take the dogs with us, Mrs White would stay at Pelham Cottage or Ormeley and sleep in my bed so that the dogs would feel a human presence under my covers at night. I was so grateful that she would do that for me, and she assured me she was happy to do so because she knew it would give me peace of mind. Of course, she adored all my dogs over the years, especially Noodle.

Rupert, Robin and India Jane all loved Mrs White unconditionally. Their favourite day of the week was Thursday, Nanny Wendy's day off, when Wags spoilt them rotten, partly for her own pleasure and partly to spite Nanny Wendy. They were given extra sweets and allowed to watch *Popeye* on the black-and-white television before bedtime, and she would then tell them lurid stories about life in the Blitz that I enjoyed as well. Jemima and Zac still remember her noisy imitations of Doodlebugs and bombs and air-raid sirens.

Mrs White tolerated Mark, I suppose, because she regarded him as a sort of extension of me, but Mark would never accept that she could not bear to be teased.

One Christmas I gave him a beautiful navy-blue cashmere dressing-gown, and when the time came for it to be cleaned Mrs White put it in the washing machine. This was surprising as she heartily disapproved of washing machines, preferring everything to be washed by hand. As a result a very small and rather sweet replica of the original emerged from the machine, still perfectly proportioned but the ideal size for a six-year-old. Mark was not pleased, and when I told him what had happened I begged him not to fly off the handle with Wags, anticipating only too well what would happen if he did.

'Morning, Mrs White,' he said a few days later, as she arrived for work. He held up the miniature. 'Would you like to have this dressing-gown for your grandson?'

At this, Mrs White flounced out of the room and out of the house and refused to come back because, in a brilliant and seamless shifting of the blame for the whole incident, she claimed that Mark had insulted her. Eventually, because life without Mrs White was pretty dismal despite the moans, I went to have tea with her in her house, and after I had consumed a great deal of humble pie and told her the whole thing was my fault – I shouldn't have bought it in the first place! – she was persuaded to return and everything went back to normal.

When I started my affair with Jimmy Goldsmith in

Wynyard Hall in County Durham, my family home, where I spent many happy years growing up with my parents, siblings and dogs.

My grandmother Edith in her Women's Legion army uniform. She wore this with huge pride at a time when there was general disapproval for service women and their uniforms.

Mark and me on our wedding day.

Mark with the infamous Help, the naughtiest dog he ever had, who spent most of his days at Pelham Cottage.

Mark, relaxed on holiday in the South of France.

Cutting the cake on Mrs White's ninetieth birthday. Zac, Jemima, Ben and I spent a happy day with her in Elmbank Nursing Home.

Aspers and Teddy with two of the baby gorillas that were housed at Howletts. Teddy knew all the wild animals that Aspers kept as he stayed there for many weekends.

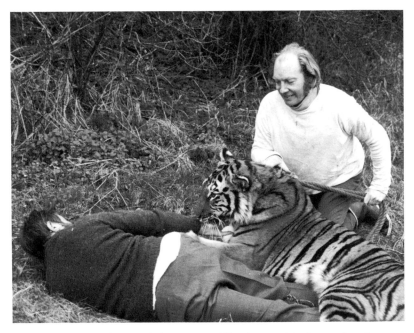

Teddy playing with one of the tigers at Howletts, with Aspers keeping a firm hold of it.

Aspers with one of his elephants

Aspers at Port Lympne eating a bit of the chocolate before giving the rest of the bar to his rhino.

Aspers with John Huston

the mid 1960s, and knowing her views on 'them that did' had only become more pronounced with the years, I was determined that Mrs White would not find out about it. But she knew me too well, and when the routine of my life altered slightly she became suspicious. Occasionally I would spend a whole night away and she knew that was totally out of character. One particular morning she arrived for work, her thunderous face already firmly in place, but I did not sense anything unusual or ominous and instead practised my usual tactic of simply trying to avoid her. However, that morning she managed to grab me by the arm outside the children's bathroom and swung me inside saying, "Ere, I want a word with you. You been carryin' on. I never thought you'd do that. I always thought you was a lady.'

As I gazed at her in horror, trying to gather my wits, she continued: 'No, it's no good trying to get out of it, My Lady, I know I done wrong but I read one of them letters you tore up and put in the basket.' Desperately trying to remember what I had put in the letter, knowing it must have been one of those you write to your lover, pouring out your heart and then deciding not to send, I quickly realised she must have read enough to be sure of her facts. I knew it was vital to make her feel it was *she* who was more in the wrong, because life with Mrs White knowing I was 'carrying on' would have been intolerable, otherwise. Drawing myself up and forgetting my grammar in the process, I said 'You done *what*?'

'I know I done wrong. I shouldn't have read the letter, but I had to know,' she stuttered.

'You done *very* wrong,' I told her firmly, and proceeded to make her feel so guilty about reading it that I soon had the upper hand.

However, I knew also that unless I made Mrs White an accomplice life would be impossible, so I sat her down on my bed and explained that Mr G. (her name for Jimmy) was really more of a platonic friend who helped me out financially and occasionally liked to take me out in the evening. Of course, sometimes he had to have 'his way', I acknowledged, but that was men for you and to keep him happy I had to submit.

At my explanation she cheered up and we had a woman-to-woman chat about how strange it was that men had to have sex, bemoaning our lot as the women who had to put up with it. From that day onwards, Mrs White became my eager collaborator, loving the intrigue and her part in it. After all, she had seen me through bad as well as good times with Mark and realised I wasn't solely to blame. She revelled so much in the secrecy of the affair that sometimes she went a bit too far, and when Jimmy telephoned she would come into the room where I was doing homework with

India Jane and my niece Cosima and hiss loudly and conspiratorially, 'It's Mr G. on the phone; I said it's Mr G., he's waiting for you.'

In 1974 I became pregnant with Jimmy's child, thirteen years after India Jane's birth. Mrs White was horrified. 'Oh, I knew you'd fallen. I could tell it by your eyes and I think it's dreadful and frankly My Lady I know you done it and I know you're going to have it, but don't expect me to even give it a look.' Needless to say, from the moment my baby Jemima was born she was never out of Mrs White's arms. It was as it had been with all my other babies, love at first sight. Jemima was followed rather too quickly by my son Zac, in 1975; and Mrs White, still expressing horror and shock, this time over how close they were in age, fell as much in love with him as she had with Jemima.

In 1980 Benjamin James was born, but by this time although Mrs White was totally integral to our lives, she had retired. I bought her a maisonette in Mortlake not far from Ormeley and there she at last lived happily with Reg. After Reg's death her usual good health began to decline and she began having dizzy spells. After several falls she broke her hip and had to go into hospital; she never really recovered her strength. I made sure that there were people to come and look after her during the day, but it was difficult to find night carers and she needed twenty-four-hour attention. I became used to her saintly neighbour George ringing me up to tell me she had had another fall, and when she broke the same hip again and returned to hospital I braced myself to tell her she would have to go into a home, for her own safety. I knew she would hate this, but she was too proud to agree to the children's and my wish that she should come to live at Ormeley with us. Eventually I found Elmbank, a lovely private nursing-home in Putney which was near enough for regular visits and where she could have her own room. I took all her favourite furniture there so that this new setting would feel comfortable and familiar.

After Mrs White was settled in the home Jemima fell in love with and became engaged to Imran Khan, the famous cricketer. I knew the press would go mad at the news and I wanted to tell Mrs White myself before she read it in the *Daily Mirror*, particularly as I had been aware for some years that Wags had considerable racist leanings. When Jemima was a baby I had employed a charming Anglo-Jamaican girl called Terry as a part-time nanny. She had been adopted by a white family in the North of England and spoke with a strong northern accent. One day I had been having lunch in the kitchen with Terry and Mrs White, with Jemima behind us in her high-chair. Terry had bought herself a wig and asked me what I thought of it. I told her that although I quite liked it, I thought her own hair suited her better. I turned to Mrs White to ask her opinion, realising the moment I did so that it was a mistake. Her false teeth chomping on a lamb cutlet, Wags looked up briefly and said, 'Me, well I prefer 'em in wigs.' Luckily, Terry had such a good sense of humour that she burst out laughing.

But I knew that telling Mrs White that her beloved Jemima was marrying a Pakistani could prove to be somewhat problematic. In fact, Robin described her as 'Alf Garnett in a frock'. The week before Jemima's engagement was to appear in the newspapers, I rang Mrs White in the nursing-home.

'Wags, do you watch much sport, I mean, like cricket?' I began tentatively.

'No, I can't be doing with that,' came the answer.

'I see,' I said rather lamely, watching one explanatory avenue close, as Wags clearly would not know that Imran was a cricketing hero.

'Wags,' I continued, in a voice full of enthusiasm. 'Guess what? Jemima is engaged to a wonderful man and Sir James and I are thrilled to bits.'

There was silence on the line.

'His name is Imran Khan,' I continued rather hesitantly.

'I see,' she said, after a pause. 'What kind of a name is that? Is he Jewish?'

'No. He's from Pakistan.'

There was an even longer silence until finally she said, 'Well, as long as she's happy.'

On the day of the wedding in June 1995 reporters and television cameras besieged the house. I arranged for Mrs White, dressed in her best, to be brought to Ormeley in a wheelchair for Jemima's wedding party. She looked so happy and was so pleased to see all the family together, and to be a part of it. Most of Imran's family thought she was Jemima's grandmother and made a big fuss of her. Before she left I pushed her wheelchair to the gate, where all the photographers were gathered as they were not allowed inside for the party, and she had her photograph taken with me by *Hello!*. She had a big smile on her face and I knew this would be an enormous boost to her morale – and definitely one up on all the old ladies in the home, most of whom she disliked intensely.

In 1996 Jemima gave birth to her first child, a son they named Sulaiman. Before his birth Jemima had promised Mrs White that she would show her the baby as soon as she came out of hospital. Shortly after Jemima and Sulaiman returned home to Ormeley, I received a telephone call from the nursing-home to say that Mrs White had had a stroke and was not expected to live through the night. When I told Jemima she burst into tears, saying, 'I can't break my promise to Wags – I must show her the baby.'

So with Sulaiman in her arms I drove Jemima to the nursing-home, where we found Mrs White lying pale and unconscious in her bed. Jemima put her tiny baby on to Wags's chest and talked to her gently, telling her his name, even though there was no response. Jemima had tears pouring down her cheeks and I too was feeling highly emotional. The next morning Helen the matron rang me to tell me that Mrs White had made a lightning recovery and was sitting up in bed having her breakfast. I rushed round to see her and she astonished me by remembering not only the visit of Jemima and the baby but also that the baby's name was 'something foreign'.

The children and I spent one last happy day with Wags, gathering round her bed to celebrate her ninetieth birthday and helping her to cut her cake. Shortly afterwards, she died peacefully in her sleep. I had wanted her to be with me through her last years, and when she died. When I had asked her to move into Ormeley where I would have taken care of her myself, even though in her later life she had lost her protective fierceness she had politely but firmly refused my offer. It pained me deeply that I couldn't look after her and see her as often as I would have liked. Thinking of her in the home, sometimes sitting alone for some hours, could reduce me to tears. I went to see her as much as I could but it wasn't the same as having her under my roof.

From the early days back in St John's Wood when I was nineteen – younger than her own daughter – Mrs White came quickly to regard me as her surrogate daughter and I came to see her as one of my closest and most special companions. My children loved her as they would a grandmother and over the years, as she mellowed, her laughter would fill our rooms. I truly loved her and there isn't a day that goes by when I don't miss her wise counsel, sitting down for a cup of tea, biscuits and a gossip at the end of the day; her stories and her take on life and our unique friendship. Sometimes I even find myself telling her things, hoping that wherever she is now she can look in and see how we are all doing. I know for sure that she would be enormously proud of all my children and grandchildren.

CHAPTER FOUR

RHODA BIRLEY

From the very first moment she entered Pelham Cottage, my mother-in-law Rhoda Birley knew it would be the right home for Mark and me, and for many years, on her visits to London, she would do everything she could to stay with us. Rhoda was a formidable woman, and while we warmed to each other almost as soon as we met she remained someone I was much in awe of – I confess now that during the early days of my marriage to Mark, when I was so unsure of myself, I was a little scared of her.

Rhoda was a fascinatingly complex woman – an Irish eccentric, a gifted artist – who with her dramatic profile and wholly idiosyncratic manner of dress was said by her great friend Maria Harrison to possess *la beauté du diable*. She was tall and slim, with wild, flowing dark hair in stark contrast to her white skin, and she had terrifyingly expressive eyes which you felt could bore right down into your soul. She dressed in her own idiosyncratic way too, sometimes very colourfully in reds and purples, a gypsy look about her and a swirling informality that was quite breathtaking, and sometimes in one of her oriental ensembles. Her daughter Maxime became a model for Dior and later a fashion designer for Chloé and Gérard Pipart, and inherited her looks and no doubt her penchant for style from Rhoda.

Rhoda was not a maternal woman, often causing Mark and Maxime confusion and emotional turbulence, but oddly she was a wonderful mother-in-law to me. There was, in her past, the fragile connection to my late mother that never failed to move me. During my parents' courtship and before their engagement my mother Romaine Combe and my father Robin Londonderry were invited to stay at Dunrobin, the beautiful hilltop castle overlooking the North Sea in Scotland that belonged to my paternal grandmother's family, the Sutherlands. Among the guests that weekend was the leading portrait painter of the day Oswald Birley, who was there to paint the Duke of Sutherland, and accompanying him was Rhoda his unusually striking wife. Many years later Rhoda told me that even though that 1920s Scottish weekend was so long ago she could still remember the beauty of my mother's voice. This was particularly poignant as in the last year of her life my mother had possessed no voice at all because of her oral cancer. It was also a revelation, as her voice had not seemed all that unique to me. I suppose we don't hear the timbre of those closest to us, and Rhoda's lovely memory of my mother having a rather special voice has remained with me.

Rhoda had married Oswald Birley in 1921, and despite a twenty-year gap in their ages they seemed to have had a reasonably happy marriage. Oswald had remained dazzled by his wife, painting her frequently during their years together. To my know-ledge Rhoda had only one big love affair outside her marriage, but the well known peer of the realm to whom she temporarily lost her heart would not leave his wife. Mark recalled the end of the affair when his mother would make dramatic and miserable appearances at the top of the staircase, her face covered in thick white powder, emphasising the tragic effect, before walking down the stairs very slowly, dragging her feet as she descended. When I first came to know her in the early 1950s, Oswald had just died and the romantic drama of her life was well in the past, but her eccentricity and passionate strength of personality had not dimmed at all.

After Oswald's death Rhoda lived on for almost another thirty years. In the late 1950s and throughout the 1960s she and Maria Harrison put on an annual festival of music and arts at her home at Charleston

Manor near Seaford – one of the prettiest houses in East Sussex – at which countless five-star performers came to participate. Many big names from the film world came without hesitation to attend Rhoda and Maria's marvellous productions, including Wolf Mankowitz, Carol Reed, Michael Denison and Dulcie Gray. These festivals were incredible feats of planning and imagination and I was in awe of Rhoda's vision, her ability to combine her bohemian outlook with well planned and executed artistic weekends. They were memorable for me not only because of the cultural highs they brought to my life but because it was at the first one I attended that I met Maria's daughter Nico, who became my sister-in-law and closest friend for many years until her tragic death.

Rhoda was greatly loved, almost revered, by all her friends, most of whom were involved in the arts. She was passionately involved at Glyndebourne and she opened my eyes to many new artistic experiences, opera being just one of them. She was, surprisingly, totally supportive of me – I saw myself in those early days as rather unformed and gauche – and she rarely criticised anything I did. On her frequent visits to Pelham Cottage, in the evenings after the children were settled and Mark was at Annabel's, we would sit together and talk. She would only settle down once she had a glass of her much loved Dubonnet (I had to get this in especially for her and stop Mark from adding gin to the bottle). She loved hearing about my childhood in Ireland and my life with my grandparents and parents. Much later, when my marriage began to disintegrate and I had started my affair with Jimmy, Rhoda loved nothing better than a good session alone with me to discuss the whole thing. Sometimes she would get perilously close to making frank enquiries about the precise detail of my and Jimmy's sex life, but to her disappointment I would swiftly change the subject. The idea of discussing something quite so intimate with Rhoda, the mother of my husband, was for me quite out of the question.

Both Rhoda and Maria were committed Christian Scientists, believing in a spiritual, prayer-based Christian healing. They were avid readers of the Christian Scientist Mary Baker Eddy, who wrote *Science and Health, with Key to the Scriptures*, a book that had a permanent place on Rhoda's bedside table. Whenever she came to Pelham Cottage out came Mrs Eddy's book, and after our little evening chats Rhoda would gently suggest that I read a bit, so sometimes at the end of the evening I would go upstairs obediently clutching the impassioned religious text under my arm. I am one of those people who cannot get to sleep without reading and I love that feeling you get after a few pages, when your eyelids start getting heavier and heavier and the book begins to slip out of your hands. Mrs Eddy's book had the opposite effect: it was so complex, the concepts so difficult to grasp if you are not a Christian Scientist, that I would guiltily slip it under my pillow and take up my own book, hoping that Rhoda would not come in to say goodnight and realise that I was never going to become a recruit to the cause so dear to her. Rhoda and Maria were clearly mesmerised by Mary Baker Eddy's teaching – and they were both, come to think of it, extremely healthy women, rarely in need of a doctor – but I never was convinced by their doctrine.

One of the more disturbing sides to Rhoda was her complex relationship with motherhood. Oddly for one so gregarious, she seemed to have no maternal instinct at all for her two children, Mark and Maxime, sending them away when very young and paying them very little attention on their return. As a result, when I first met Mark he was, understandably, lacking in family feeling. Gradually, however, through our marriage, the arrival of his own children and a sequence of much loved dogs, he began to learn how to show the affection he had been denied as a child. When I got to know Rhoda I was embarking on motherhood; from day one, I adored my children and could never spend *enough* time with them. We were polar opposites in this respect and I must admit that when Mark told me stories of his childhood, Rhoda's treatment of him and Maxime truly disturbed me. I used to wonder what it was about her past or her own internal make-up that had made her this way. Even when Mark was an adult, Rhoda would behave in a bizarre fashion towards her only son, convinced, she said, that sometimes he had the devil in him. Whenever they had an argument and he turned his back, she would silently make the sign of the cross as if to exorcise the demons in him. Sensing her gesticulations behind him, he would suddenly round on her as if in a game of grandmother's footsteps; this habit of Rhoda's both infuriated and deeply upset him.

Rhoda was, though, rather sweet with all her grandchildren and a much better grandmother than mother – when I urged Rupert, Robin and India Jane to finish up all their food at mealtimes she would admonish me for being too strict. Perhaps, then, maternal love had simply skipped a generation. I was, as I have mentioned, rather in awe of her, and at my age and stage in life I couldn't be judgemental. In those days it would have been impossible to ask someone of the older generation about their innermost feelings or past traumas, and so you had to accept someone for what they were, difficult as that sometimes could be.

Right from the outset Rhoda made me feel good

about myself, and when, at the beginning of my marriage, I was insular and shy and shut-down at times, she showed me great warmth; and during her stays at Pelham Cottage she was flatteringly curious about the way I did things, particularly as regards make-up and hair. In the 1960s hairstyles were very much the thing and Rhoda was fascinated by my hairpieces. These long swatches, often made of real hair, were the equivalent of today's hair extensions, except that hairpieces were rather difficult to keep in place; it took a great number of hairpins to do so and could become embarrassing when things got a bit steamy and you had to take them off at the culmination of a romantic night out.

The fashion for back-combing particularly enthralled her and she envied me a technique and dexterity that I used on my own hair, in truth no more dextrous than any other girl's in the 1960s – we all did our hair in the same way. Rhoda would ask me rather shyly if I would do her hair and somewhat reluctantly I would agree, aware of my total lack of qualifications as a hairdresser as I stood behind her trying to give some height to her hair. At one stage of the operation she would invariably look rather like a hedgehog until I had smoothed it down. For a brief and perfect moment the effect was stunning, but then Rhoda would fiddle with the precarious edifice until it flopped and became as flat as it had been at the beginning.

She never minded if it didn't look right at the back, although I would insist to her that the back was just as important as the front. The front posed its own problems: I never knew whether to incorporate the two little horns of hair that curled inward on either side of her forehead – usually I left them alone and I am afraid they looked rather incongruous and abandoned.

Rhoda was also intrigued by my eye pencil, although she never used one herself and would instead opt for the rather strange practice of covering her face in very white make-up which looked like a layer of wet cement. Once, aged around five, Robin announced in a rather too loud whisper that Ami's face (the children's name for their grandmother) looked 'like tissue paper'. At night the white mask would be cleaned off with a powerful and camphor-smelling removal liquid called Ejyra, produced by Mrs Field, a friend of Rhoda and Maria's, and they both absolutely swore by it: everything about the Ejyra removal lotion was admirable and its cleansing properties were second to none. But the Ejyra night cream that Rhoda liberally slapped on her face every evening before bed made her look as if she had just emerged from a bog; her whole bedroom stank of the stuff. The cream was so thick and glutinous that all her pillowcases were saturated with it and you could even smell it in the corridors outside her bedroom. You always knew when she had been staying at Pelham Cottage – the smell pervaded the air for days afterwards and reminded us so much, often quite joyfully, of her presence.

Rhoda was quite often my saviour, and while I often got her ready for parties, she also helped me. There was one memorable weekend when Mark and I were invited to a big party at the Brighton Pavilion. We were staying the night of the party at Charleston, where I arrived in advance to change into my dress before setting off for the evening. Knowing how hopeless my memory was, before leaving London I carefully checked that I had packed the right shoes, the right bag, the right jewels, the right stockings. Unfortunately, however, I forgot to take the most important item, Maxime's beautiful model-size dress that she had given me especially for the occasion.

In extreme distress I rushed into Rhoda's camphor-reeking bedroom wailing: 'An awful thing has happened, Rhoda. I've left my dress behind and it's too late to get Mark to bring it as he has already left London. What on earth shall I do?' After a short pause she opened her wardrobe. 'Well, darling, as it happens I have just the answer,' she said, smiling at me. 'Maxime gave me a couple of dresses the other day that are much too tight for me – Balmain, I think. Come and try this one on.' And she produced from her cupboard a ravishing dress, white with a touch of pink, and I pulled it over my head while Jackie, Rhoda's long-suffering maid, zipped it up. Then I looked in the mirror and thought, 'Hang on a minute – there's something wrong here.' The waist was beautifully nipped in, the skirt was full and sumptuous, the whole thing was a perfect fit but the entire front was missing. The dress was cut to reveal a substantial expanse of me, right down to below my bra. I should mention here that bras were never my strong point and could more accurately be described as functional rather than sexy. On that particular day the standard had dropped even further than usual: I was wearing a relic – a kind of maternity bra. Turning to face Rhoda I said, 'Rhoda, I think there's a panel missing.'

She took one look at me and said dismissively, 'Oh no, no darling, it's meant to be like that.'

'It can't be meant to be like that, Rhoda. My entire bra is showing.'

'Don't be silly,' she said, 'it's very attractive like that. You know, you're a young girl. It's nice to show it off, and nowadays it's just the thing to show off a bit of bra too.'

'I can't possibly go like this, Rhoda,' I objected, looking aghast at her suggestion. 'I might just as well go with nothing on at all.' But Rhoda was adamant.

'Doesn't she look wonderful, Jackie?' she asked, inviting confirmation from her maid, who was looking just as appalled at the sight as I was.

Jackie and I exchanged looks; we both knew that not only did I not look wonderful, I looked absolutely grotesque. We slunk quietly out of the room, and without telling her employer Jackie came to the rescue and found a chiffon scarf which she cleverly sewed in place to cover up the front bit. 'Oh, you've ruined it!' said Rhoda when she saw Jackie's handiwork. 'It was so much prettier before.'

However, safely fichued in I went to the ball, and during the evening I whipped off a bit of the scarf to show my cousin Patrick Plunket how frightful I would have looked. He thought Rhoda was hilarious but somewhat mad, and in some ways he was right, but for me she had a heart of gold.

Rhoda was an inspirational cook. Her food was the stuff of legends and she would famously feed Lobster Thermidor to her roses. As Maxime once explained: 'She would make fish stew and sometimes forget that she was making it for the garden, so she would add a bit of cognac, some garlic and spices. The roses would almost cry out with pleasure.' Maxime went on to inherit her mother's eccentricities in the food department and became well known herself for the meals she used to cook for Andy Warhol and his followers. At the start of my marriage I was a terrible cook and so on her visits Rhoda would rustle up mouth-watering meals, but whenever I asked her for the recipe she could never supply it because she invented it as she went along. My kitchen would be a hive of activity, every pan would be brought out as with her long fingers she threw in ingredients, stirring them vigorously with a wooden spoon. Even her coffee was amazing, made to some secret formula in a saucepan; it was a breakfast ritual and I have never tasted coffee like it – it was absolutely delicious. I think Mark learned about the importance and excellence of food from Rhoda, and perhaps the greatest compliment he could have paid his distant and critical mother was to incorporate her flair and standards for cooking into his nightclubs and restaurants.

When I came out of hospital in 1961, having just had India Jane, my longed-for daughter, I was still only twenty-six and had slight postnatal blues. Rhoda was there for me on my return home. We had lost our au pair at Christmas after she had gone mad and tried to knife me – a very distressing day at Pelham Cottage – and had just employed Irene, a young Portuguese girl who happened to arrive for her first day of work on the day of my homecoming. Neither Irene nor her husband was able to speak a word of English. I burst into tears as I tried to explain what

I needed, but Rhoda, who had brought me home from the hospital, started trying to teach Irene how to make scrambled eggs. Irene, still wearing her hat and coat, got more and more confused and, to Rhoda's puzzlement, through my tears I began to laugh hysterically. 'You're wonderful,' I said to her. 'Wonderful, but quite mad.'

I saw less of Rhoda when we moved from Pelham Cottage, and she died when I was in my mid-forties. As I grew older and more experienced and sure of myself, I wished she had lived longer. I would have asked her things that I did not dare ask her earlier, and attempted to understand her more. There were some interesting revelations about Rhoda in a recent obituary of Maxime, ranging from her delightful eccentricity – adding a new room to Charleston merely to serve as a setting for posing some Ballets Russes dancers, cooking for the roses – to her darker side: the 'maternal storms' that scared Mark and Maxime throughout their child-hoods, and her dispatching of Maxime alone to America after she was 'invalided out' of the WRAF for rebelliousness, telling her, 'We have no room for you in our home.'

I used to go to Charleston to see Rhoda in her later years, and although towards the end of her life she was disorientated and somewhat muddled, she was always pleased to see me and we spent some peaceful times together. Rhoda died in 1980 and is buried in the churchyard at West Dean Church in Sussex, next to Mark's father Oswald.

CHAPTER FIVE

JOHN ASPINALL

I have been lucky enough to have had some marvellous holidays during my life, but nothing has ever thrilled and excited me as much as the first one Mark and I went on in 1962 with our adored friend Aspers – John Aspinall – and his first wife, Jane. Even the invitation itself was delivered in an unconventional, electrifying way: close to midnight Aspers, followed by Jane, burst into our bedroom at Pelham Cottage. Jumping on to the end of our bed, they shook the bedcovers off to make sure we were awake, then commanded: 'You're coming on holiday with us!' Bleary-eyed, we emerged from sleep to learn that the couple who were supposed to be going with them had dropped out and we were lucky enough to be drafted in. They were proposing to take us on a safari in Kenya. Those three weeks turned out to be a huge adventure and a memorable turning point in my life.

Up to then, I had only ever been as far as the South

of France and never away in winter, so the thought of going as far as Africa filled me with excitement. Aspers and Jane were constant guests at Pelham Cottage and were as much at home there as we were, so after they had made us get up we all went downstairs and the rest of the night was spent planning our escapade.

The safari was magical. To be taken to Africa to see animals in their natural habitat was exciting enough, but to be taken by Aspers was an unbelievable privilege. The trip was made all the more special by his guide, a rather irresponsible Austrian called Heini Demmer who had no qualms about getting too close to some of the wildlife, even allowing us, encouraged by Aspers, to be chased by an angry rhino. I loved cooking and eating around the campfire and then retiring to the tent for an early bedtime. We spent most nights sleeping under canvas, and this was enormously pleasurable to me. Waking around 5.30 a.m. and looking out from the tent at the breathtaking sunrises over Kilimanjaro was an experience that lives with me still. The sense of space, the majesty of the landscape and the exhilaration of seeing the animals in those vast expanses have never left me, and I have been back several times since then, often taking people for their very first time and so able to catch their initial excitement as Aspers did with me. I do remember that Mark was not so enchanted; he found the whole business of living in a tent highly uncomfortable, and spent most of his time in camp sitting in a chair drinking bottle after bottle of Beehive brandy and making as few excursions as possible.

That holiday cemented my friendship with Aspers and Jane that had begun several years earlier. I can still hear the amusing way he came to describe our first meeting, which had occurred when I was nineteen and newly married to Mark: 'There I stood, a blond Nordic god, and Annabel, who was rather beautiful herself in those days, was spellbound.' While I didn't actually see him as a god, I did find him quite unique, and almost immediately was overwhelmed by the brilliance of his storytelling. He regaled me with a tale called 'The Pearl' which went on for ages. Aspers was renowned for his long-winded but amusing stories, and I never tired of hearing them.

One of his favourites turned on the discovery that Aspers was not, as he had always been led to believe, the biological son of Robert Aspinall, the British Army surgeon who had brought him up. It was during his mid-twenties that he found out that in fact he was the son of a soldier named George Bruce. He loved to tell this particular story – and he was so good at setting the scene: his mother had had a romantic liaison with an Army officer after a dance and he had been con-ceived under a tamarisk tree in India, where he was born in 1926. When I first heard this, I asked him if he had been shocked by the discovery. 'Far from it!' he smiled, and proceeded to tell me of his mission to find his real father and of their ensuing friendship. Aspers was very close to his mother – the wonderful Lady Osborne, known to us all as Lady O – and she was a great presence in his life.

Aspers loved Pelham Cottage, so much so that it became a sort of second home to him and he was forever popping in and out. Actually, he liked it so much that he frequently colluded with Mark in coming up with plans for the incessant home improvements that were part of our daily living. There came a time when I began to long for a life without builders, but with Aspers's constant intervention I could not envisage when that dream might become a reality.

Quite apart from instilling in me a thirst for adventure, a craving to experience new things and see new places, Aspers was my inspiration and guide to the wonderment and beauty of animals. Up until meeting him, my knowledge of them, apart from my love of dogs, had been confined to adoring them from afar, but Aspers awakened in me a deep respect and thrill for wildlife that came to shape me for the rest of my life. Of course, his great love for wild animals and the enormous contribution he made to their welfare have been well documented, and his legacy lives on to this day.

I was there at the beginning, when Aspers started to keep wild animals in his flat in Lyall Street in Belgravia. Rescuing them from a miserable and life-threatening existence, he had taken in Tara, a baby tiger, and Deddy, a capuchin monkey, and until he was able to relocate them to the country he would often be seen walking them on a lead in the streets around Eaton Square. I thought he was an exceptional person to have taken these animals in and I loved to visit and spend time with them.

In the hectic 1960s, when acceptable boundaries and social codes really were being widened, I don't think I knew anyone more eccentric and wildly passionate about things than Aspers. And it was this passion for two massively contrasting elements in his life that enabled him to make his mark. One of these stemmed from his love – and in his case, it should be said, talent – for gambling.

From his undergraduate days at Oxford he was determined to set up a casino that would rival in elegance and reputation the gambling venues of the eighteenth century. However, he was, until 1960, thwarted by the illegality of gambling in Britain and so was unable to start up anything officially. Instead, he used to hold private gambling parties every ten days to which Mark and I and his other friends would all go. It wasn't too long before these parties became immensely grand, attracting some of the biggest gamblers in the country. Lady O would provide the buffet supper; her game pie and fabulous desserts were renowned and Aspers's gambling friends knew her affectionately as 'Al Capone with a shopping basket'.

In order to avoid discovery, Aspers was very careful to change the venue for each game, which on some occasions used to take place in Claus von Bülow's flat and on others at various friends' houses. It was because of these infamous gambling evenings that a subsequent court case led to the creation and passing of the 1960 Gaming Act – known informally as 'Aspinall's Law' – and the ensuing legalisation of gambling in Britain. I remember the legendary party in a flat near Hyde Park that led to this monumental change. We had been playing my favourite game, chemin de fer, but as Mark and I had decided to go home early, we just missed the raid by the police. By all accounts it was quite dramatic and all the players – that evening, a grand total of twenty-one members of the nobility – were arrested and taken to the local police station.

After the legislation was passed Aspers was able to go above ground, and before long he opened his gambling club at 44 Berkeley Square which came to be known as the Clermont Club. There, halfway up the beautiful baroque staircase, was the celebrated Grand Salon where you could play chemin de fer, roulette, blackjack and, of course, backgammon. A few years later, with Annabel's in the basement, the combined activities of 44 Berkeley Square had made it the most fashionable, if hedonistic, address in London. At the time, I didn't realise quite what an iconic place it had become and didn't truly appreciate how lovely it was of Mark to have named Annabel's after me.

Nowadays I am often asked if I am the Annabel of Annabel's, and when I reply it is with a huge amount of pride and honour. I used to love going there and had many memorable nights both upstairs and downstairs. So many well known, interesting people passed through the club – one night I ran a winning bank while sitting beside Ian Fleming, as Frank Sinatra hovered behind my shoulder. Everyone came to the Clermont: I would often see old friends like Bill Stirling, Archie Stirling, Simon Fraser and Sunny Marlborough (the 11th Duke), and among other regulars – I do not mean people who merely popped in for a few hours' gambling, interspersed maybe with a dance downstairs – was Lord Lucan, known to his friends as Lucky. Rarely did I walk into the Clermont and not see Lucan sitting at a table playing backgammon. Little did we anticipate the scandal with which he would be synonymous – to me he was simply part of the furniture.

Of course, Aspers's predominant passion was for

animals, in particular mammals, for which he had an affinity almost unrivalled in documented relationships between man and beast. It was after a successful bet that he was able to purchase Howletts, a beautiful Palladian house near Canterbury, which was to become the home of his first zoo. Later he was able to buy another zoo at Port Lympne near Hythe, also in Kent, and together with the Clermont Club these places brought him fame and notoriety. His two worlds were not, after all, unconnected, since one paid for the other: the income from his gambling pursuits provided the funds which fed and housed hundreds of animals, many of whom he saved from extinction.

I was one of the earliest and most regular visitors to Howletts. Here I got my first taste of what it was like to live closely with gorillas and I loved walking through the woods with Aspers, accompanied by both adult and baby gorillas. The older ones could be quite rough when trying to play and would drag you behind a tree by your hair. I soon found that the best way to prevent this was to carry the smallest gorilla on my shoulders, thus guaranteeing a more peaceful walk. But all this rough-housing was done in friendship; they were simply boisterous adolescents. I developed a quite remarkable affinity with Noushka, a wolf cub who used to follow me around, one weekend coming to my room and pilfering things from my bag.

Of course, later, when Robin at the age of twelve was mercilessly mauled by Zorra, a tigress in the early stages of pregnancy, we were shattered by the ferocity of the savage attack. Robin had been nervous and Zorra had sensed this and had herself been threatened by Robin's height. She sprang on him, bringing him to the ground, and fastened her jaws around his head. It was only the heroic intervention of Aspers and his second wife Min that saved his life. While Aspers prised the animal's jaws open, Min held on to her back legs to prevent her from ripping Robin's body, as tigers do to their prey. For years afterwards I was riddled with guilt over letting Robin into that enclosure, but I had had total trust in Aspers who, of course, did not know that Zorra was pregnant and so catastrophically unpredictable in her behaviour.

Aspers absolutely loved boats and he invited us to go on the first boat he ever chartered, which took us round the South of France and Corsica. After a week he was becoming increasingly irritated by one of the stewards, who used to mince round the table, muttering under his breath. Unable to bear his attitude, and after repeated warnings, Aspers threw him overboard when the boat was anchored in Cannes harbour. Thankfully, he was able to climb straight up the ladder again and was definitely less bolshie thereafter.

Aspers was hugely sociable and well read, and I knew

that with this combination of attributes he and my brother Alastair would get along well. In 1962, their first meeting culminated in an agreement to share the expenses of a yachting trip round the Greek islands, on which Mark and I were also invited. Alastair and Aspers very soon realised they were kindred spirits, even though Alastair did not gamble. Both of them were confirmed bibliophiles, sharing a passion for Rider Haggard and Oscar Wilde. Alastair soon started calling him Macumazahn ('he who keeps a bright lookout at night'), the name given by the Zulus to Allan Quatermain, the hero of *King Solomon's Mines* and Aspers's hero too, even if he was a hunter. Following this pattern, they started referring to unpleasant people as Zikali, the name of a malevolent African dwarf who also appeared in several novels by Haggard.

This trip proved to be full of adventures, including the accidental gate-crashing of a circumcision party in Gallipoli. Later, Aspers would tell everyone that I refused to explore the islands, preferring instead to sunbathe on deck, but however addicted to the sun I might have been, sightseeing with Aspers as a guide was irresistible as he made it such fun. One evening we all piled into a restaurant where, encouraged by me, he broke into a loud rendition of his favourite song, 'Marta, Rambling Rose of the Wild Woods'. He became so carried away by his singing and our applause that he continued to sing it on the balcony of the restaurant and we were all arrested by the local police.

Like his literary guru Haggard, Aspers, as I've mentioned, was a great storyteller, admitting proudly to being an 'incontinent orator'; whether the stories were true or embellished never seemed to matter. Two that he particularly enjoyed telling concerned Alastair. Aspers invited Alastair and Jimmy's brother Teddy for a safari in the Okavango Game Reserve in Botswana in southern Africa. Teddy, the founder of *The Ecologist* magazine, had never met Alastair before and they became close friends, sharing a tent in which each night they would talk well into the small hours covering every conceivable subject that a polymath like Teddy had at his fingertips. Absorbing though the participants found these conversations to be, the rest of their safari companions heard them only as an unending monotonous drone that kept them awake, night after night. Action was called for.

During one particularly long nocturnal discussion, Alastair and Teddy broke off their talk when they heard a loud scratching on the side of the tent. For a split second they feared that a hungry lion was about to burst in. Their fears were soon dispelled by a bellow of laughter, and by Aspers bounding into their tent. Exasperated by the drone, he had decided to frighten them into silence. For a natural raconteur like Aspers these circumstances were gold dust, and thenceforth the description of what he had seen that night in the tent became increasingly inflated. The best version had two terrified figures standing with their backs to the tent, preparing to defend themselves with the first objects they could grasp: in Alastair's case, a book on Hittite footwear and in Teddy's a book on Herero ancestor worship! Teddy also loomed quite large in Aspers's more extravagant flights of fancy: he imagined him as the leader of a legendary Afro-Jewish tribe, the Bajewaqui, which would one day rise again to re-establish its once glorious empire.

However, despite the jokes and high jinks that characterised the safaris, Africa remained a place of fundamental importance to Aspers, particularly through the Zulu nation, whose aspirations for democratic and economic welfare he championed for many years. The Zulu politician Mangosuthu Buthelezi, who with Nelson Mandela helped lead the long fight against apartheid, regarded his friendship with Aspers as something 'so precious'. In particular Buthelezi admired Aspers for his understanding of the perils of imposing Western governmental styles on the complex reality of Africa. 'He loved Africa,' Buthelezi once said, 'for what it is and what it can be, not for what one would want it to be.'

My favourite of all Alastair's and Aspers's stories

concerns a visit that Aspers made to the ancestral home of the Londonderrys, Wynyard Hall. Not finding a driver to collect him at Darlington station, Aspers made his way to the house. On arriving he rang the bell, then, after the umpteenth cavernous ring he pushed open the huge front door, which creaked ominously. There was no sign of life. Sweeping aside the festoons of cobwebs, he made his way through endless corridors and rooms until he came to the enormous ballroom where he found the '9th Marquess' (Alastair's title) huddled by a primus stove and surrounded by a pack of famished bulldogs, growlingly intent on sharing their master's meagre rations. The only word of truth in this surreal story is that Alastair and I forgot to meet Aspers at the station.

For all his make-believe, though, Aspers could also deliver wisdom and insight. In 1972 Jimmy started talking about wanting to have children with me. Although my affair with him had started in 1964, I was still technically married to Mark but living separately. At first I was too frightened to even contemplate the idea. I knew that if I became pregnant the news would get into the papers and make headlines. I was also terrified of what my maternal relations would say and certain that my cousin Patrick, whose opinion meant so much to me, would disapprove. Aspers and Jimmy were best friends and talked frequently to each other.

A year or so later, I found myself walking around Howletts with Aspers. He told me that I was making a terrible mistake, that Jimmy was desperate to have more children and, addressing me rather as if I were a Siberian tigress, he said, 'It's time you mated with Jimmy and gave him the children he wants.' He tried to explain that I should consider it a great honour that Jimmy should want to have children with me, adding rather forbiddingly: 'If you don't do this soon, one day the affair will be over and you will be left with nothing.'

I thought long and hard about this advice and began to understand the value of the commitment that Jimmy was offering me. I concluded that when a man asks a woman to have his child it is a wonderful thing. In 1974 our darling Jemima was born and I had the greatest difficulty keeping Jimmy and Aspers out of the room while I was having her, so excited were they both by the event. Aspers became chief godfather and, being an atheist, albeit having his own religion and his own creed, we had a rather unusual christening – more of a naming ceremony – in the garden at Pelham Cottage. I can still see Aspers holding Jemima up high in the air and making his moving speech welcoming her into the world.

Jimmy's and Aspers's very close relationship went back as far as Jimmy's early exit from Eton, aged sixteen, when they met through his older brother

Teddy. Hardly a day went by without lengthy conversations between them; most of these would take
place while Jimmy was having breakfast in bed early in
the morning. They would discuss every subject under
the sun, even though they were probably going to
meet for dinner that evening. When Jimmy finally
succumbed to the cancer that claimed his life, Aspers
was inconsolable, and I don't think he ever really recovered from his soulmate's early death.

Shortly afterwards he was struck down with cancer
of the jaw, and throughout his long illness he showed
the same courage as Jimmy had; he never lost his sense
of humour, nor the pleasure he took in his daily visits
to his animals. With his face swathed in bandages, he
would clamber over the gorilla enclosures, feeding and
talking to them, helped by his third wife Sally Curzon
and his children. Sally nursed him devotedly, hardly
ever leaving his side. He hated spending any time in
hospital, despite his many visitors and the home-
cooked meals Sally would bring in for him. I would
visit him at home in London and at Howletts and
when he was well enough we would talk and reminisce
and he would tell me how much he missed Jimmy.
Like Jimmy he was unbelievably uncomplaining.

Aspers died in June 2000, aged seventy-four. I do
not envisage ever meeting anyone quite like him again
in my lifetime. He was a man of vision, a man full of

energy and drive, and he left a lasting legacy to the fabric of British life. He is remembered for so much: his enormous contribution to wildlife, his zoos, his pivotal part in the changing of the gambling laws and his eccentric take on life. Like everyone else I remember him for these things, but I am also privileged to have known him as a close friend and confidant, to have spent adventurous holidays in his company, to have heard his stories and been amused by his wit, dazzled by his electric presence.

If Aspers knew that I was writing this about him, I feel sure he would tell me to discard it all and just bring his beliefs about wildlife to the page. So I am ending here by outlining the creed that he drew up. I find it exceptionally moving:

I believe a wildlifer must not expect to be rewarded with recognition or worldly approval. His work will be to him his recompense. Only in his own peace of mind and self-esteem will he find solace.

I believe in *jus animalium*, the rights of beasts, and *jus herbarum*, the rights of plants. The rights exist as they have always existed, to live and let live. I believe in the Buddhist concept of *ahimsa* – justice for all animate things. I believe in the greatest happiness for the greatest number of species of fauna and flora that the Earth can sustain without resultant deterioration of habitat and depletion of natural resources.

I believe in the sanctity of the life systems, not in *the sanctity of human life alone.* The concept of sanctity of human life is the most damaging sophism that philosophy has ever propagated – it has rooted well. Its corollary – a belief in the insanctity of species other than man – is the cause of that damage. The destruction of this idea is a prerequisite for survival.

I believe that wilderness is Earth's greatest treasure. Wilderness is the bank on which all cheques are drawn. I believe our debt to nature is total, our willingness to pay anything back on account barely discernible. I believe that unless we recognise this debt and renegotiate it, we write our own epitaph.

I believe that there is an outside chance to save the Earth and most of its tenants. This outside chance must be grasped with gambler's hands.

I believe that terrible risks must be taken and terrible passions roused before these ends can hope to be accomplished. If a system is facing extreme pressures, only extreme counter-pressures are relevant, let alone likely to prove effective.

I believe that all who subscribe to these testaments must act now, stand up and be counted. What friends Nature has, Nature needs.

CHAPTER SIX

PATRICK PLUNKET

The other day after spending the weekend in Kent, I was driving home through the Wealden lanes – signposted rather delightfully in the spring by the RAC as 'the Cherry Blossom Route' – and as I passed the turning to West Malling I was transported back to The Mount, Patrick Plunket's glorious pale-pink home. Some of my happiest times have been spent there, and memories came flooding back through the open car window as I drove by. I realised that only Pelham Cottage had come close to bringing me as much excitement and contentment as had The Mount. For a long time during my life I had never felt anywhere to be as special as Patrick's family home, and it was only when I settled in Pelham Cottage that I felt I had recreated anything like the cherished atmosphere of the place.

The Mount had been a sanctuary for me, and during my teenage years had provided a treasured contrast to my own home. At a time when the relentless gloom that had surrounded my mother's slow death had profoundly affected us all – especially my father, who had begun to drink heavily – Patrick's home, open to us unconditionally, was bright, sparkly and spontaneous. It was a free yet safe place, lived in by adults who were not that much older than me.

Patrick, born in 1923, was the eldest of three brothers, all of whom were my childhood heroes. Their parents – my parents' best friends – had been killed in 1937 in a plane crash on their way to visit the American newspaper proprietor William Randolph Hearst, and so they were brought up largely by their father's brother, Uncle Kiwa. I stayed there regularly until well after my marriage to Mark, and I mostly recall the endless laughing. At The Mount the gaiety seemed to come up through the floorboards; in spite of the tragedy of great loss, it was almost as if the carpets were laid on an underfelt of mirth. Partly this was due to Uncle Kiwa, a benign, smiley, craggy-faced man who had a slightly disconcerting habit of adopting the Buddhist lotus position and sitting cross-legged for hours, beaming and radiating calm and happiness. He was an eccentric old soul who had a profound influence on the boys. I remember always being in awe of him – his distance from the centre of activity in the house detached him somewhat from the everyday – and a little tongue-tied in his presence.

I adored the flower-filled rooms and the uncomplicated yet stylish ways of The Mount. Patrick was glamorous, a perfectionist, and even while embarking on his career as a courtier he was always modest about his rather elevated role. I will never forget the way he broke the news to me that we were related, and have always been grateful for his tact and compassion.

Aged seventeen, I developed a tremendous crush on his brother Shaun, and though he was in love with Genevicve François-Poncet, a girl for whom I used to devise rather cruel imaginary mishaps, I thought I could detect an undercurrent of mildly flirtatious encouragement from Shaun. One weekend I caught Patrick watching us both with a concerned look, and later I confronted Shaun with what could be worrying Patrick. Shaun became most uncomfortable and carried on reading his book, muttering that I should ask Patrick myself; so later that night on the way back to London in his car, in response to my questioning, Patrick at last told me the whole romantic truth of my paternal grandfather's love affair with Fannie Ward, one of the sensationally lovely, Edwardian Gaiety Girls. Six weeks after my grandparents were married, she had given birth to a daughter, Dorothé, and with impressive magnanimity my grandmother Edith had brought the child to live at Mount Stewart, their home in Northern Ireland. Strange as it seems, she did not enlighten her own children of their relationship to Dorothé but it came out eventually – though, bafflingly, had been kept a secret from me and my siblings. At seventeen Dorothé had married Teddy Plunket and had three sons – Patrick, Robin and Shaun, and as a result Patrick and I were indeed first cousins. I was shocked at this revelation. If I hadn't asked then, when would I have been told? I often wonder if I would have been kept in the dark for ever. Secrets in families are dangerous things.

After realigning myself – for while I knew my crush on Shaun was not going to lead anywhere I did continue to have feelings for him, even after receiving this news – I felt immensely privileged that the Plunket boys and I were related. When I reach back through the years I have an indelible image of Patrick in my mind: tall, impeccably dressed, a voice full of merriment, his eyes crinkled up in laughter. He radiated an irrepressible sense of fun and a delightfully flattering absorption in conversation, even with the biggest bores – though he certainly had plenty to say about those bores when they were out of sight. His easy-going manner – the antithesis of the stuffy courtier – and a unique sense of humour, combined with his respect for her position, had made him a deeply valued confidant of Queen Elizabeth.

On the death of George VI in 1952, Patrick had

become an equerry to the new Queen, and he adored her from the outset. They enjoyed a very special connection, and a year after the coronation he was promoted to the position of Deputy Master of the Queen's Household, the royal servant in charge of all royal servants – not only those employed at Buckingham Palace but also those who worked under the housekeepers responsible for the other royal residences, at Sandringham, Windsor, Balmoral and even Holyrood House in Scotland. Among his duties, Patrick oversaw with apparently effortless flair the endless entertaining of visiting heads of state as well as the domestic social commitments that the monarch is required to undertake.

Three years the Queen's senior, Patrick provided the continuity that she badly needed after the death of her beloved father, and he became one of her chief supports and advisers for nearly the first quarter-century of her reign. In his biography *The Queen* Ben Pimlott describes Patrick's role as a cross between an elder brother and the best Jeeves of all time; but he was so much more than that, having been born with his own distinctive aristocratic style and charm.

The respect for the institution of monarchy and its titular head was mixed with a refreshing irreverence and fun to which the Queen herself responded. He was recognised as the one member of her staff who could talk to her on equal terms. He told me an amusing story that illustrated their exchanges. One day when the Queen came to lunch at The Mount, Patrick proudly showed her the just completed portrait of himself by Graham Sutherland. He had thought himself cutting rather a debonair dash, choosing to wear for the portrait a favourite pale-blue cotton polo-necked sweater, the get-up of the moment in the 1960s, but the Queen had no hesitation in enquiring with a bemused look why Patrick had opted to be painted dressed as a dentist. There was clearly an openness and honesty between them based on genuine respect, friendship, even teasing. I doubt, however, that she made fun of his hair as we did: despite his good looks Patrick was sensitive about its rather coarse texture, and although he combed it as smoothly as he could, we did tease him about it looking a bit like a lavatory brush. He did not find this funny.

The Mount was full of fun, and some of the things we did back then survived into my life in Kensington, including our love for making home movies. I particularly remember Shaun's productions, which were all called on to be in, and one stands out in the archive of my memory. 'The West Malling Bank Robbery' was filmed after lunch one Sunday when we all dressed up in outfits cobbled together from various corners of the house, complete with pistols, masks and swag-bags. Patrick and his friend David Airlie were convincingly menacing as robbers, with thick beards, black highwayman masks and old, tightly belted macs. David's wife Ginny and another female guest were deliciously amusing as vampishly decadent molls, with their thickly painted crimson lips.

Action! David drove Patrick's car at top speed down West Malling High Street, screeching to a halt outside the National Westminster Bank – at which moment Shaun, behind the camera, suddenly spotted the local policeman approaching on his bike. Secretly hoping that a bit of drama and unexpected verisimilitude in the shape of a real arrest was about to be injected into the production, Shaun trained the camera on the officer, but to his disappointment the policeman barely took his foot off the pedal – just kept on cycling blithely past us.

'Mornin' all. Having a good time?' he called out, with a cheery wave and an indulgent smile, as if to say, 'Grown-ups will be children.' Little did he know that he had missed out on helping to create the eye-catching headline, of 'Royal equerry and lady-in-waiting arrested for attempted bank robbery'. Another weekend the guests were roped in to re-enact the famous French film *Rififi*, in which the hero-villain was Jules Dassin, France's and the 1950s' answer to George Clooney.

With the benefit of being able to look back on these times, I see how important they were in shaping me, in forming the way I was to run a house; and even if all this happened at a subconscious level – no one *instructed* me on how to be hospitable – I feel sure now that I learned a lot, perhaps just by being at The Mount and in the relaxed, good-natured, generous company of Patrick and his brothers. Later, when Patrick moved to his grace-and-favour apartment, he would come and spend time with us at Pelham Cottage. Not only was he enchanted by the house and garden but I think he also tuned into an atmosphere not unlike that of The Mount. I know too that he could feel my own sense of security and peace living there, and while he was essentially a rather unemotional and detached man, my happiness and wellbeing were important to him, which touched me.

Patrick was a genius at making places feel beautiful and lived-in. Whenever he walked through the door of Pelham Cottage he would go straight to the flowers that might be sitting in a vase in the hall or sitting-room. Mark used to like flowers to be tipped into a vase looking as if they were natural and wild but this was anathema to Patrick, who was well known for his spectacular, rather formal, flower arrangements, and I can still hear his giggle as he would take the flowers out, then place them back in the vase deftly and exquisitely rearranging them. Sometimes Mark would know that Patrick had called round just from the look of the hall flowers. Actually Mark and Patrick got along extremely well – each acknowledged in the other a love of antiques and they had similar good taste and style in the way they furnished and decorated interiors.

If Patrick wasn't able to come round to see me for a while, he would call me to give me an update on how his life was at the Palace. He loved the huge banquets put on there and once, his laughter bursting down the telephone wires from the Palace to Pelham Cottage, he confided that a large sticky bun had been found stuffed down the side of a sofa with a full set of false teeth embedded in it. We had great fun trying to work out who they belonged to!

Patrick was a great protector. He was quietly supportive and he exuded an immensely reassuring sense of concerned authority and also warmth – an invaluable comfort when I was on the brink of losing a parent. For many years, although Alastair held the Londonderry title after Daddy's death, he was so young that my sister Jane and I thought of Patrick as the head of our family. As my father lay dying and we children stood around his bed, he suddenly became confused and mistook my sister Jane for Patrick, holding her hand and imploring her to take care of us all. I think

I understand how protected he must have made the Queen feel.

During the final months of his life Patrick was yet again sitting for a portrait, this time by John Ward. The sessions took place at Pelham Cottage and I would drive him back to his apartment, knowing how ill he must be feeling but also aware of his absolute refusal to show it and thereby give in to the pain. He never once admitted to anyone that he knew he had cancer, although he did intimate to me that he hoped this wasn't the case; and he used to throw away his medicine. Ten days before his death, and determined not to believe the evidence of the severity of his illness, he left his room at King Edward VII Hospital in Beaumont Street and went to the Palace to oversee a particularly important dinner. This astonishing, slightly mad act did not go unrecognised. I was told that in the morning on his breakfast tray was a perfect posy of miniature spring flowers and a handwritten note from the Queen herself.

I went to visit Patrick in hospital as frequently as I could and would sit by his bed and try to make him laugh – our relationship had been characterised by mutual enjoyment and humour, and I wanted his last days to be good ones for him. On one of my last visits before he died, he said to me: 'Annabel darling, promise me you won't sell Pelham Cottage', and although

I nodded, I felt terribly guilty because I had already sold it and was about to move to Ormeley. I have often thought about that false promise but in the years since have consoled myself with the thought that Patrick would have absolutely loved Ormeley Lodge, with its glorious garden and my own happiness here too.

Patrick died far too young, at Easter 1975. Glancing round at the funeral I saw a look of such sadness on the Queen's face that I had to look away at once for fear it would bring out my own tears that I was struggling to hold back. I minded losing him so dreadfully. Only two families were present in the tiny Chapel Royal: ours and a complete gathering of the British royals. Had Patrick not died, I truly believe he would have been there to help Diana. I think he would have taken her dancing, given her wise counsel and provided her with the guidance that she so desperately needed. Perhaps the most symbolic and revealing detail of the importance of Patrick Plunket in the life of the Queen lies simply in the place where he is buried: the royal family's own private burial ground at Frogmore in Windsor Park, close to the Castle.

One of the Ladies of the Bedchamber believes that 'One of the great tragedies of the Queen's life was the death of Patrick Plunket'. Indeed, with his passing, some of the jauntiness and light went out of her life, and a good measure disappeared then from my own life as well.

CHAPTER SEVEN

EDITH, MARCHIONESS OF LONDONDERRY – MAMA

It is one of my deepest regrets that my paternal grandmother, Edith, did not live longer into my adulthood. I would have been thrilled for her to have known my children as they grew up and for them to have heard about her incredibly interesting and varied life. She did get to spend a little time with Rupert and Robin in their very early years but, sadly, she died in 1959, aged eighty, having battled bravely against cancer. She left a lasting legacy – through her ideals, her pioneering work during the First World War, her dazzling social life, her reputation as a superb hostess and her marvellously inspired and vibrant gardens – and lives on through the many books and articles written about her, as well of course, through our family's collective memories.

My grandmother, affectionately known as Mama, played a very important part in my life. Jane, Alastair and I spent a great deal of our childhood, particularly when we were very young, at Mama and Papa's magnificent home in Northern Ireland, and we returned there for several holidays when we were older. She was a captivating woman, and from a child's perspective her immediate fascination lay in the mysterious snake that coiled first around her ankle and then curled further up her leg until it disappeared beneath her pale-blue silk dressing-gown. We were mesmerised by the sight of it and spent hours discussing it amongst ourselves – we had never seen a tattoo before. Even when I knew that she had acquired it on a trip to Japan with my grandfather and he had had one done on his forearm, it lost none of its fascination for me. Whenever I sat with her on my bed at Mount Stewart, trying my hardest, at her insistence, to learn the catechism by heart, I would try and take a peek at it. She told me later that as hemlines rose after the First World War her snake became a talking point among press photographers, who at first mistook the tattoo for a new fashion in patterned stockings.

Mama was tall with a very straight back that made her a somewhat intimidating figure to us children. And despite the universal view that she was a great beauty, we could not share in the opinion. We all thought she looked rather like a sheep. The pack of snapping and yapping and occasionally nipping Pekinese that followed her everywhere added to her formidable image.

Now when I see paintings of her, I think she was rather beautiful in a stately kind of way. She was a talented storyteller, and I used to love it when she read to us from her fairy story *The Magic Inkpot* that she had written and published for her youngest daughter Mairi. I can still hear her bringing life to the mysterious creature that lived in the pot, telling us of his adventures with Robin my father and Mairi in the familiar Irish landscape that surrounded Mount Stewart. I still have a copy of the book and reread it from time to time – my grandmother had a wonderful imagination, and recently I have felt inspired to write stories for my own grandchildren.

Those early pre-war years spent at Mount Stewart on the edge of the beautiful Strangford Lough, framed by the Mourne Mountains, retain for me a magical quality. The house was long and of grey stone, its edges softened by billowing ivy. It had been built by the first Viscount Castlereagh whose son, the second Viscount – and Foreign Secretary from 1812 to 1822 – was responsible for masterminding the end of the Napoleonic Wars. Inside were the same red leather chairs on which he had sat with the Allied sovereigns in 1815 to thrash out the details of the Congress of Vienna. These, and the glorious Stubbs painting of the famous racehorse Hambletonian, were just some of the treasures past which I used to rush on my way through

93

the black-and-white chequered marble hall. Life inside Mount Stewart had remained as grand as it had been before the First World War: the staff included a butler, several footmen, the housekeeper, the cook, innumerable housemaids, a telephonist to man the busy exchange and a hospital nurse. The house was filled with the entrancing smell of the potpourri that Mama made herself and during the early spring the intoxicating scent from large baskets of hyacinths wafted through the huge downstairs rooms.

But it was life outside Mama's house that dictated our *Swallows and Amazons* existence. Wearing little more than bathing suits in those sunny summers before the Second World War, we built dams on the stream in the wood, tumbled over abandoned boats on the beach, raced each other through the lanes on our bicycles and went for long rides on our chubby, long-haired black ponies. During the long hot months Mama would swim at night in her salt-water pool. Crossing the lawn after dinner by the light of the moon, she would remove all her clothes and plunge into the water. When my sister Jane and I had reached our early teens we were invited one day to join her, and clad in our dressing-gowns and bathing-suits we followed her to the pool; we had promised each other that we wouldn't laugh, but when we emerged from the changing huts we were both seized with such appalling giggles that we were never asked to accompany Mama there again.

As the wife of my grandfather, the 7th Marquess of Londonderry, Mama was a political hostess well known for inviting all the great names of the day to her celebrated parties at Londonderry House. Up to two thousand guests would assemble at the eighteenth-century mansion at the corner of Park Lane, never forgetting their first sight of the hostess. Wearing the fabulous Londonderry jewels, and reminiscent, some thought, of a Christmas tree, Mama would stand to greet them at the top of the enormous staircase. On particularly crowded nights, it could take twenty minutes to reach her. Edith had grown up in grand society, coming from a distinguished aristocratic background herself. She well recalled watching her own grandmother, the Duchess of Sutherland, dressed in grey velvet and with a diamond tiara on her head, on her way to Buckingham Palace to fulfil her duties as Queen Victoria's Mistress of the Robes.

Mama remained a vivid presence throughout my schooldays. During the war we lived in a house near Brookwood in Surrey called the Brown House where, in order to supplement the rationing allowances, we kept chickens. One day my grandmother came for a visit bringing with her three bantams as a present for Jane, Alastair and me; there were two hens and one cockerel and they were extremely pretty with their black and gold feathers – I called mine Josie. Alastair decided he had to call his Jesus, which infuriated my grandmother who threatened to take it away unless he changed the name. Jane and I promised Mama that we would persuade him to change the name as soon as she'd gone. But Alastair refused to be budged and Jesus spent his war strutting round the chicken pen keeping a beady eye on his harem.

Only when I was grown up did I begin to realise the full extent of Mama's strong personality. She had accepted Papa's love-child Dorothé with such dignity and inner strength – not an easy thing to do. I knew that she and my grandfather had not approved of my mother, Romaine Combe, and had made life extremely difficult for my father when he told them he intended to marry her. My mother came from a large close-knit family and had met Daddy in October 1930 at Dunrobin Castle in the northern Highlands of Scotland, my grandmother's family home, where she had been invited by my father's sister Maureen. I have always felt that the injection of Combe blood was the best thing that ever happened to the Londonderry men and, happily, as the marriage endured and she began to recognise my mother's many qualities, Edith softened. Her initial frostiness took quite some time to thaw, though, and I wouldn't have wanted to be on the receiving end of it. My mother was a strong woman to have been able to look past it and behave as courteously and tactfully as she did with my grandparents.

Eventually, my mother earned Mama's outright respect for the patience with which she handled my father Robin's increasing dependency on alcohol. My grandmother was as distressed as everyone else when my mother was diagnosed with cancer. Aware that she was dying and wanting to show me her grandmotherly support, Mama visited me at my tutorial college in Oxford. She offered quite a spectacle, driving down the High Street in her chauffeured Rolls-Royce and scooping me up for a slap-up lunch at the Randolph Hotel. I remember her kindness, but what sticks in my mind is the most welcome five-pound note she pressed wordlessly into my hand just before she left. When my mother died so young, my grandmother was deeply upset. I was saddened when my father refused to see her, following my mother's death. So bereft and shattered in his grief, he acted harshly, his anger with my grandparents for having been so hostile to her rushing back to him. For my part, I think he was wrong about this – Mummy was really rather fond of Mama, and in later years especially.

Tragically, Mama also long outlived her son, for my father died four years after my mother, leaving Jane, Alastair and me orphaned. I was twenty-one.

I remember the misery of his funeral at Wynyard. The only light-hearted moment came when after a particularly chewy forkful of food Mama's false teeth fell out of her mouth and under the table, where the dogs immediately fell upon them – hoping, no doubt, that what had just dropped might be a particularly delicious piece of roast beef.

I am enormously proud that my grandmother made a significant contribution to the increasing prominence of women in the first half of the twentieth century. Edith was a woman ahead of her time, not a feminist, exactly, but someone who believed that women should be acknowledged for the important contribution they could make to public life. Her charm and her ability to get on with people from all backgrounds and of all ages made her immensely popular. She was a much loved friend to many, some becoming members of the private club that she named the Ark. Included were some of the grandest figures in the country, all of whom adopted a codename by which to be known: Churchill became Winston the Warlock, Nancy Astor, the first woman Member of Parliament, was Nancy the Gnat, and the painter William Orpen took the title Orpen the Ortolan. Edith herself was Circe the Sorceress of classical mythology – appropriate for my grandmother in recognition of the number of people who had been bewitched by her.

The Conservative Party was grateful that Edith's considerable gifts were directed their way, as she proved an invaluable campaigner on their behalf. However, she also cherished her close and much speculated-upon friendships with the portrait photographer Laszlo and Ramsay MacDonald, the Labour Prime Minister in 1924 and again from 1929 to 1935. The historian Brian Masters described their relationship as being made up of 'the lightest feather of flirtation and the deepest flow of affection' and there were always rumours about the exact degree of their closeness, but in her auto-biography, *Retrospect*, published in 1938, Edith ex-plained the basis of her fascination for the man: 'He was an old-fashioned socialist who loved beautiful things, dignity, dinner parties and dressing up in resplendent uniforms. He was simple and naïve, the only genuine pacifist I have ever met.'

Mama worked hard for the suffragette cause and fully endorsed it, although she distanced herself from the more violent tone of their campaigns. She was impressed by the heroic part that women played during and after the First World War and had founded the Women's Legion in 1915, for which she was awarded the honour Dame of the British Empire. She saw that the energy generated by the suffragettes might well be dissipated when the conflict began and was determined not to let this happen. The Women's Legion capitalised on that emancipated force and became the largest entirely voluntary body during the war. A measure of the organisation's seriousness was indicated in the adoption of a military-style uniform, including a bronze badge showing the figure of Victory with a laurel wreath – the badge was known by members as 'the lady with the frying pan'. The women were employed in a variety of work from heavy farming including hay-making and ploughing, to catering for the convalescent camps. My grandmother's pioneering organisation had an undeniable influence on the government, not least in their decision to give women an official role in the second part of the war.

Mama wore her Women's Legion uniform with pride, despite the fact that there was considerable prejudice against servicewomen and their uniforms. On occasion she found herself forced out of lifts by porters who wanted to express their disapproval at the masculinity of her dress. One day when we were having tea at the Randolph she told me about her amusing encounter when lunching one day at a friend's grand house. Her story made me roar with laughter:

On ringing the bell the parlour maid regarded me with suspicion. I thought I must have come to the wrong door, and said, 'Is Lady So-and-so not in?'

'Yes,' replied the maid. 'If you will go down by the

area and give me a message I will see if Lady – will see you. She is very busy, and has company to lunch.'

I then gave my name. I could see she was shocked and horrified. When I left after luncheon the maid asked to be excused, adding, 'I thought you was one of them 'orrible Army women.'

My grandmother was a deep-thinking woman, a visionary. She wrote in her memoir:

Every day now we read of fresh exploits in those spheres [inequality], since the ban of sex has been removed, we need not feel surprised that women's new status of equality has come to stay. What is really surprising is that they have achieved so much in such a short space of time. We have still to see the advent of the businesswoman here on a large scale, as in America, where women are employed in banks and businesses in very responsible positions. We have yet to see a woman Prime Minister and Ambassador, but every day, in spite of opposition, more and more women are entering new professions.

She went on to explain that she believed women would make excellent diplomats and, were she alive today, she would have been delighted to see them in all positions of high political authority. She drew the line only at careers in the Church: 'Women have already great scope for much-needed work as deaconesses in which they are doing noble work, but this is an entirely different question from the idea of women being ordained as priests. To use no stronger phraseology, it would be most inexpedient and unseemly.'

Only four months before her death Edith was still giving parties. Harold Macmillan was the final Prime Minister to attend a glittering reception at London-derry House, as the guest of honour on Mama's eightieth birthday. Except for members of the suffragette movement, only a minority of women of her generation held such emancipated views. I cannot help feeling that she would have got on extremely well with Lady Thatcher, for whom I am sure she would have thrown one of her dazzling parties.

Among her other attributes was her considerable talent for gardening, and she became known as one of Ireland's greatest practitioners of the art. The series of beautiful gardens that Mama made at Mount Stewart – the Italian Garden, the Spanish Garden and the Shamrock Garden (planted out in the shape of the Irish leaf) – all held a particular enchantment, and she left me with a lifelong love of flowers both wild and cultivated. It was the wild garden at Mount Stewart that I especially loved, and the wild garden at Ormeley Lodge with its meadow flowers and the butterflies that it attracts is my favourite patch and where today I still feel close to my grandmother.

Sadly, Mama was not able to visit Pelham Cottage as much as either of us would have liked as she had been suffering from cancer for almost two years when we bought it and had become very frail. But we were able to share the cottage with her a few times when we first moved in, and although it must have seemed very small to her, used as she was to big houses, she told me that she found it very pretty and gave me ideas about what to do with the garden, which I welcomed.

It is a deep source of regret to me that I did not spend more time with Mama when I was an adult. I was so young and preoccupied with my small children in the years before she died. I think that, with more maturity and self-assurance, I would have been able to ask her so much more about her life and her thinking.

When Jimmy died, amongst the waves of sadness came the realisation that I had lost a person whose opinion on so many subjects I valued hugely. I used to ask him so much, loved to listen to his opinions on so many topics, and I so miss his intelligent world-view, being able to share thoughts, listen to his interpretation of events. In the same way I regret, with the insight into life that I have now acquired, not having had the time to ask my grandmother more. I see now just how far ahead of her time she was. An inspirational woman, she achieved so much in her life. Even to the end she continued her work for the Red Cross, another of her commitments. She is buried at Mount Stewart next to my grandfather in the part of the garden where the creature from *The Magic Inkpot* and his friends used to dance together. I have met many intriguing people in my life, but I cannot think of a greater joy than the chance to travel back in time and sit in her garden discussing the world with my extraordinary grandmother.

CHAPTER EIGHT

GEOFFREY KEATING

Wandering around Ascot racecourse, lost, feeling out of place and wishing I had some money to back a horse I had taken a fancy to, I bumped into Geoffrey Keating. Beaming with bonhomie, he took me under his wing and lent me a ten-shilling note. I was seventeen at the time and although he was a friend of my sister Jane, this was my first meeting with him. He was witty and clever and charming, full of wonderful stories, and that special afternoon spent with him is still etched in my mind. Little did I know then that Geoffrey would later become one of Mark's and my closest friends, and a constant dropper-in at Pelham Cottage.

There has never in my life, before or since that Ascot day in 1951, been anyone remotely resembling Geoffrey. Eccentric would not be the right word to describe him – maybe outrageous would be nearer the mark. He was like a bouncy ball – irrepressible and full of beans – and his big smile would always light up a room.

After that afternoon in Ascot, at least two years elapsed before I met Geoffrey again, by which time I was married to Mark and had settled at the cottage. Geoffrey lived in a small house in Three Kings Yard, off Davies Street in Mayfair, and he soon became a constant friend. He came into our lives permanently as a result, really, of his love for my sister Jane. She was absolutely stunning, rumoured to be the most sought-after single woman in London and he, like many other men, was deeply enthralled by her; but unfortunately for him, his feeling was unrequited.

I loved it when Jane came to stay at Pelham Cottage and I was only too happy to include her in my family life, particularly to be with the children whom she adored. After the death of our mother, Jane had had to assume responsibilities that were way beyond the call of duty, especially given Daddy's problems. She had had to run Wynyard, perform duties in the local community and take care of Alastair and me. So I was extremely pleased that at Pelham Cottage the roles were reversed and I could look after her. It was not exactly an arduous task – we adored each other (and still do) – and I loved entertaining her friends.

Geoffrey was immensely gregarious – he collected extraordinary people around him, always sharing new friends with his old ones. He soon established himself as a regular visitor to our home, popping in through the back gate at any time of the day. I vividly remember arriving home one day to find a beaming Geoffrey emerging from the house to greet me with the words, 'I have a couple of people for you to meet; they're waiting in the study.' And there, to my total surprise, in front of me in the tiny study of Pelham Cottage were the distinguished and controversial Israeli military leader, Moshe Dayan – as ever, wearing his trademark black eye-patch – and his daughter Yael, then rapidly establishing herself as a novelist. Despite the eminence of these unexpected visitors, whom I never met again, I somehow took it all in my stride, something I doubt I would be able to do today.

The ubiquitous Geoffrey was always accompanied by a beautiful young woman and sometimes, in the midst of looking after my small children, the presence of these gorgeous, seemingly unburdened and rather perfect women in Pelham Cottage was a touch irksome, especially if I was upstairs settling the children and could hear Mark and Geoffrey downstairs talking and laughing with them. One evening I came down to find that Geoffrey had brought round a young and stunning Stefanie Powers – much to Mark's delight!

One of the most fascinating characters that Geoffrey knew was the American humorist S. J. Perelman, and well aware that he was one of my heroes one day he brought him unannounced to Pelham Cottage. Sydney

Joseph Perelman was one of the writers of the Marx Brothers' scripts *Horse Feathers* and *Monkey Business*, and also of the Academy Award-winning screenplay for *Around the World in Eighty Days*, and it was his connection with the Marx Brothers that entranced me. I had seen every one of their films over and over again (I still laugh at them today). Perelman even reminded me of Groucho Marx, with his impressive repartee, and it was thanks to him and Geoffrey that I finally met that even greater hero – Groucho Marx himself. My father once told me of his disappointment when he was introduced to one of his favourite authors, John Buchan, whom he had found to be boring in conversation. But to my delight, Groucho was just as funny in real life as he was on the screen, his repartee just as sharp as in his films.

Occasionally Geoffrey and I would have a disagreement, and Mark had a love-hate relationship with him, but however many times we fell out, nearly always over trivialities, the rift was always swiftly mended and, within a heartbeat, Geoffrey would reinstate himself at Pelham Cottage. He could be very direct, and sometimes this got him into trouble. He once incensed Mark so much that he ordered Geoffrey out of the house. It was early evening, and Mark had been supervising the laying down of a new Persian carpet. Geoffrey appeared in the hall, and taking him by the arm Mark led him proudly to the newly carpeted area. 'Well?' he asked. 'Do you like it?' 'No. Not at all,' said Geoffrey. Mark was so furious that he grabbed him and practically threw him into the garden. It took him some time to calm down. However, a couple of days later Geoffrey was back, as though nothing had happened.

Geoffrey was someone who invariably managed to infuriate and then charm one out of a bad mood. Whenever I was cross with him he would come up with some ridiculous comment, which never failed to amuse me. 'There may be *non non* on your lips, but there is always *oui oui* in your eyes.' Sometimes, though, I would find one of his statements incredibly frustrating. He once scolded Jane and me: 'The trouble with you two,' he remarked, 'is that your way of solving a problem is to say "Be reasonable and see it my way".' I expect, with hindsight, that sometimes he was right, but I felt defensive when he lectured me or told me off and didn't really take on board what he was telling me.

With the exception of his wartime exploits I knew very little about Geoffrey's background when I first met him, but I was soon to discover his surprising depths and talents. He was Irish, born in 1914, the son of Hannah and Matthew Keating. Geoffrey's illustrious father was the first Irish Member of Parliament to be elected to the House Commons at Westminster, representing the Irish Parliamentary Party from 1909 to 1918.

Geoffrey embarked on a distinguished career in Fleet Street, beginning with a job on the *Daily Sketch*. During the Second World War he joined Allied Newspapers, then after a stint in the Territorial Army 60th Rifle Brigade he was appointed public relations officer to the British Expeditionary Force in France. Later he moved to the Middle East where he became a conducting officer for war correspondents. Geoffrey's exceptional gifts as a photographer were acknowledged when he was made head of the Film and Photography Unit of the Eighth Army. He was soon regarded as an outstanding war photographer and celebrated for his patriotic photographs of Field Marshal Montgomery, with whom he formed a close professional association. His pictures of Monty in the desert handing out cigarettes to the troops managed to transform the general's rather stiff and uncharismatic image into one of national hero back home.

His work, along with that of other distinguished cameramen and war correspondents including Alan Whicker, was credited with presenting the British Army's achievements in battle to the world. Geoffrey remained close to his wartime colleagues, and in 1974 Edward Ardizzone, who was made official War Artist in 1940, wrote a fascinating book called *Diary of a War*

Artist in which he pays tribute to Geoffrey, praising his skill and thanking him for making 'my job as a War Artist a feasible one'.

Geoffrey often spoke movingly and sensitively about his wartime exploits, and the time he spent in Italy with Alan Whicker proved to be a particularly daring episode in both of their lives. As prisoners in 1943 during the Germans' control of the beachhead at Anzio, they made a pact together that if the Germans maintained the upper hand they would both make a run for Rome dressed in some tattered gardening clothes that they had found in an old shed. Luckily this contingency plan proved unnecessary, as eventually the US Fifth Army arrived from southern Italy, bringing liberation to all the troops including Alan and Geoffrey.

Wounded on several occasions, once after taking a direct shot in the head, Geoffrey was commended for his lack of fear and awarded the Military Cross at Tobruk. His war tales, in particular the story of his own possibly apocryphal moment of triumph when he liberated the Italian residents of Monte Cassino from the Germans single-handed, became legendary. But he could also be serious: we learned a lot from him, and we never tired of hearing about his wartime experiences. After the war Geoffrey joined BP, working initially in Persia but then in the 1950s returning to work for them in London.

Geoffrey was a bit of a dark horse, keeping certain aspects of his character hidden from even his closest friends. For example, I never knew whether he had had a problem with alcohol as a young man, because when I met him he was teetotal and only ever drank soft drinks. However, this practice of temperance had changed by the early 1970s, by which time he was indulging in drinking binges and would get wildly drunk. Mark remembered him sitting at the bar at Annabel's as if he owned the place, and never fearing the consequences of his behaviour, drunk or sober. Whenever things got out of hand, and in particular after he had insulted whole parties of Arabs, the staff developed a procedure for getting him out. One of the doormen used to walk him home through Berkeley Square and as they passed the J. Walter Thompson building Geoffrey would stop, undo his flies, and pee into the letter-box – with great accuracy, all over JWT's expensive doormat. After that he would be quite happy, and go home like a lamb. Although Mark continued to row with him from time to time, he always adored him.

Much as I loved Geoffrey I never imagined he would settle down, so I was amazed when in the early 1970s he married Susie Shafto. Susie was wonderfully laid back and obviously understood Geoffrey better than any of us. I was delighted and honoured when they invited me to be a godmother to their daughter Rima. Geoffrey was totally besotted with his daughter and was a devoted father; I used to love seeing them together.

He was also a prudent investor in property, and as well as snapping up most of the houses and flats in Three Kings Yard he bought a small flat in Tuscany – at Porto Ercole, a fashionable little port where many affluent Italians had their summer villas. From the pictures he had taken, I could see that Porto Ercole possessed enormous charm, with brightly coloured fishing boats moored in the harbour and small painted houses dotted around the port. The flat itself was right in the centre, above the Yacht Club marina. One summer, when I had left it too late to find a holiday villa, Geoffrey offered to rent me his flat. I was grateful and relieved, but when we arrived I could see that while the flat was undoubtedly appealing, it was not suitable for a family the size of mine. But Rupert and Robin and their friend Nicholas Hildyard were happy enough to squash into a makeshift dormitory in the semi-converted store room on the ground floor, while India Jane, myself and our nanny slept upstairs. To start with, the boys thought it was all rather an adventure, but unfortunately the small lavatory next to their bedroom was used by anyone in the port who cared to drop in, and consequently the smell became increasingly bad.

Upstairs, the flat was immensely chic, but in no time at all everything that could go wrong with the plumbing, went wrong.

Thinking I was rather competently taking matters into my own hands, I found a plumber, but then failed to understand his rapidly delivered instructions. In fact, my Italian was more or less non-existent, so I completely missed the warning he gave after he had completed his repairs, that on no account were we to flush the loos or turn on the taps for twenty-four hours. A few hours later, when the first loo was flushed, the entire plumbing waste of Geoffrey's flat descended through the floor into the Yacht Club's kitchen, landing on their preparations for their annual gala evening. Although Mark later found my description of the incident hysterically funny, the Yacht Club's owner did not, and only after much cajoling from Geoffrey plus a generous handout was he finally appeased. Geoffrey was as usual very protective of me and took the blame himself.

Never neglecting his wartime talent for taking pictures, Geoffrey would whip out his camera at the slightest opportunity and take totally unposed photographs. I have hundreds of the children and some poignant ones of my adored friend and sister-in-law Nico, who tragically died so young. Today, the walls of my bathroom are adorned with his photos, and the atmosphere evoked in these shots – the honesty of the moment – can in an instant transport me back to the times when they were taken.

Geoffrey remained a dear true friend to me through all my turbulent times. He embraced Jimmy as a friend while never losing his long-standing friendship with Mark. Geoffrey died in 1981, and I still hear hilarious stories about him.

One of the funniest was told to me by Jonathan Aitken concerning a journey he took with Geoffrey to Abu Dhabi in the 1970s. Once on board the plane, Geoffrey insisted on introducing himself to every important-looking first-class passenger on the Middle East Airlines flight with the whispered words, 'I am Jim Slater's and Jonathan Aitken's *homme de confiance*.' Because he delivered this self-description with increasing unsteadiness and frequency as their journey to the Gulf progressed, the principal recipients of his message were not best pleased. Geoffrey's targets were five or six eminent City of London bankers who, at the request of the Foreign Office, were acting as advisers to the Abu Dhabi Investment Authority (ADIA), then the largest sovereign wealth fund in the world. Even in the early 1970s it had millions of surplus petrodollars to invest. Slater Walker, the investment company Jim Slater launched with the Conservative MP Peter Walker in 1964, was keen to win a slice of the ADIA action so had engaged Geoffrey as their consultant because he knew the Gulf well from his days at BP. To put it mildly, he was an unconventional Middle East adviser.

Geoffrey of Arabia was good on the ground with his Abu Dhabian acquaintances, but in the air with blue-blooded bankers his behaviour was counterproductive. One of them tried to shut him up by warning that Slater Walker's investment proposals would not figure on ADIA's agenda if he went on being such a nuisance. Another asked the stewardess to insist that Mr Keating resume his seat. Both remarks were met with bellicose shouts of disapproval and erratic hand gestures which might have been interpreted as Geoffrey's first moves in a bout of fisticuffs. At this point Jonathan thought it prudent to restrain Geoffrey, who mercifully fell into a deep sleep in the seat beside him. After landing, though, he assumed the curious posture of a greyhound crouching in the slips. Then at the tannoy command of 'Doors to manual!' he catapulted himself up the aisle elbowing everyone else aside and yelling 'I'll fix that bloody agenda!'

By these tactics Geoffrey arrived at the top of the aircraft steps ahead of all the other travellers. Catching sight of the line-up of sheikhs assembled on the tarmac as the ADIA reception committee, he yodelled them a greeting in his pidgin Arabic, waved enthusiastically, and executed what might loosely be described as the opening steps of an Irish jig. Continuing the choreography of this dance was too much for him. He now tripped, and tumbled head over heels down the stairway, bashing his bald head against step after step in his agonising descent until crash-landing in a bloodstained heap at the feet of His Excellency Sheikh Mohammed Habroush, Chairman of ADIA.

'Hello, Hairbrush,' hiccuped Geoffrey, 'I am Jim Shlater's *homme de confiance* and this is his top man Mishter Jonathan Aitken who is a candidate for Parliament and will shoon be an MP.' A figure of considerable avoirdupois, Geoffrey struggled to his feet and attempted to embrace the sheikh, who was small in stature. They both fell over. Geoffrey's bloodstains spread across the white silk dishdash of his host, who from his horizontal position now called for medical assistance.

Geoffrey thought this a good moment to tell a joke. 'Can you tell the difference between me and a Dublin tart?' he asked, continuing in the same breath: 'She's hauled on the bed and had as a matter of course. I'm bald on the head and mad as a hatter of course.' Sheikh Mohammed Habroush pretended to find this uproariously funny. ADIA's official interpreter did his best to convey the wit and wisdom of 'Sir Geoffrey' (a title he had bestowed on himself during an earlier visit) to the assembled Arab dignitaries, albeit with a translation which required an ingenious performance in mime.

By this time the scene on the tarmac was bearing more than a passing resemblance to the Mad Hatter's Tea Party. The eminent City of London bankers had to be patient and watch it from the top of the arrival steps. Stretcher-bearers arrived and carried Geoffrey to the VIP lounge. Sheikh Mohammed Habroush gallantly insisted on escorting his wounded friend there. As Jonathan and his colleagues sat in a private room while sticking plaster was applied to Geoffrey, the latter hissed at him, 'Tell Hairbrush what Slater Walker wants from ADIA and get him to put it on top of the bloody agenda at tomorrow's meeting.' So he did. ADIA later allocated substantial funds to Slater Walker for investment in property. This was a big breakthrough at the time. It would not have been achieved without Geoffrey, a most unusual consultant who never gave his friends and colleagues a dull moment.

One evening in 1981 Geoffrey rang me in Richmond to see if I wanted to come up and have dinner at Three Kings Yard. I told him I couldn't as it was very foggy and I was afraid to drive in those conditions. Geoffrey was used to my reluctance to drive up to London at night, and I profoundly hope that he believed me because the next morning he dropped dead from a heart attack. It was a terrible blow and I still miss him as much today as I did then; Geoffrey understood the meaning of friendship.

During the last few months of his life when Mark was ill and in and out of hospital, we would talk a lot about Geoffrey and what a gap his death had left in both our lives. Sometimes we imagined him striding through the hospital doors, smiling and bouncy as ever, commanding 'Come on! Get out of that bed and do your physio. I'm expecting to have dinner with you at Mark's Club this time next week.' And we both agreed that, with his infectious love of life, Geoffrey was indeed the one person Mark would have obeyed if he had been around. I miss Geoffrey still, and only wish he had taken one of those marvellous photos of himself, capturing his wide grin and his *joie de vivre*, so that he could join the wall of memories he created for me.

CHAPTER NINE

CLAUS VON BÜLOW

I first met Claus von Bülow in 1957 at one of John Aspinall's weekly gambling games. He was a tall, elegant, somewhat saturnine figure and he spoke in a distinctively drawling voice. Extremely erudite in his manner, he gave a brilliantly false impression of superiority – Claus does not actually possess an ounce of haughtiness – and we spoke of some play he had enjoyed. He has always been knowledgeable and highly cultured in his artistic pursuits, and even today I still go to see plays that he recommends.

Claus and Mark set off a spark in each other and the three of us soon became great friends. Claus became almost immediately a regular visitor at our house at no. 9 Halsey Street and then later at Pelham Cottage. I could tell from upstairs if Claus was in the house – the endless rattle of the backgammon dice was a give-away as he and Mark were compulsive players. I used to talk to Claus in between games and was fascinated to discover that my Londonderry family and the von Bülows had known each other well in the previous generation. Claus was born in 1926 in Copenhagen and grew up in Denmark. In 1939 my father's sister Maureen and her husband Oliver Stanley, who at the time was President of the Board of Trade (the equivalent today of Minister of Trade), had visited Denmark on a governmental mission. Here they met Claus's grandfather, Fritz von Bülow, a former leader of the Danish Upper House and a government minister.

When Germany invaded Norway and Denmark in April 1940, Claus's mother, by now a good friend of Maureen's, was in England staying at Claridge's (where she had arranged to meet her secret lover) and Claus was stranded at his boarding school in Denmark. Oliver was a member of Churchill's war cabinet, and he arranged a seat on the special diplomatic flight for Ionna von Bülow to be reunited with her fourteen-year-old son. This was an exceptionally generous act, as the diplomatic courier flight was much in demand, having only four passenger seats. Two years later the von Bülow family were again indebted to Oliver when he helped Claus to apply to Cambridge University and secured him an introduction to the historian Professor G. M. Trevelyan, then Master of Trinity College. Claus was so bright and articulate – his English was impeccable despite Danish being his mother tongue – that although he was only sixteen he was offered a place at Trinity College to read law. Claus still speaks of his gratitude to 'my Uncle Oliver'. Having made the most of his time at Cambridge, Claus attended the École des Sciences Politiques in Paris – he was fluent in French as well – and after passing his bar finals gained a place in Lord Hailsham's legal chambers.

Claus – or Clausikins as he came to be affectionately known to us – was always immaculately dressed and shod, and often when he came to Pelham Cottage he was accompanied by the most ravishing girls, all eyed rather lustfully by Mark. Claus, Mark and our great friend Mark Brocklehurst had a running competition to see who could acquire the snuggest, shiniest and smartest shoes, all made by a certain Mr Cleverley. Mr Cleverley's shoes fitted so snugly that they made walking almost impossible. Claus always maintained that it was those shoes that forced Mark to earn enough money to enable him to afford a chauffeur.

For some time, Claus lived in a rather beautiful flat in Belgrave Square. It had a small annexe that Jimmy and I rented for a short time after we began our affair. Occasionally if I arrived early at the flat, I would ring Claus and suggest he came over for a chat. Direct access between the flats was blocked, but it was possible for Claus to get into the annexe via his kitchen. One evening Claus came over, wearing bedroom slippers and his dressing-gown. Shortly afterwards Jimmy joined us, and out came the backgammon board. After about half an hour, Claus announced he had to go as he was having dinner at Annabel's with Mark. Shortly after his departure there was the sound of loud banging, and a furious Claus reappeared to tell us that he had been locked out. Knights, his gay butler, having failed to notice Claus's departure, had gone out for the evening and locked the kitchen door. He was now in a quandary: it was too late to cancel his dinner with Mark, which meant that a quick search through Jimmy's wardrobe for something to wear was the only solution.

But this posed its own problems for Claus; for many years there had been something of a sartorial competition (not just concerning shoes) going on between him and Mark – a field of endeavour foreign to Jimmy, who was quite without any of these vanities and, at this stage of his life, although always tidy, was not at all clothes-conscious. When Claus slipped into one of Jimmy's jackets he looked so ridiculous that I was soon weeping with laughter. Although both men were roughly the same height, Jimmy was more heavily built than Claus, far broader in the shoulders, and his jacket made Claus look like an American football player. There was something about Claus's narrow, aristocratic, aquiline face arising atop these huge shoulders that was totally absurd. Also, the trousers were baggy and too long – but this proved a mercy, because worse was to come. Claus could hardly join Mark wearing his bedroom slippers and was therefore forced to don a pair of Jimmy's shoes, which were at least two sizes too large and as unlike a pair of Mr Cleverley's as you are likely to see. As Jimmy and I continued to howl with mirth Claus shuffled sadly and uncomfortably off for his rendezvous with Mark.

The next day Claus told me that halfway through dinner Mark had leant across the table and said, 'You really have got to speak to Davies & Son about those shoulders' – they shared the same tailor – 'they are appalling.' When, as they got up to leave, Mark shot a contemptuous glance at Jimmy's supertanker footwear, Claus feared that his club membership would be revoked forthwith.

In 1965 Claus fell in love with an American heiress, Sunny von Auersperg, who had two children by a previous marriage. When I first met her, I liked her instantly. She was charming and gentle and the two of them adored each other. A seemingly fairy-tale couple, they married a year later and came to live in London, and it was shortly after this that Claus wanted his annexe for Sunny's German maid – the same maid who, as it turned out, heartily disliked Claus and was later to betray him so dreadfully at his trial. So Jimmy and I had to move out.

A few years later Claus and Sunny moved to New York. Claus had started working for Paul Getty Senior in 1959, and now, unable to follow his legal career, he continued to do so. He soon became so indispensable that in his memoirs Getty describes Claus as his 'right arm'. Sunny and he had a daughter, Cosima, and her birth brought Claus tremendous joy. I used to see Claus and Sunny when Jimmy and I were visiting New York on one of his business trips, often taking Jemima and Zac with us. They adored Cosima and we would go for long walks in Central Park, then back to their exquisite apartment on Fifth Avenue. I would also make sure each time I was in New York that I spent at least one lunchtime with Claus at the Carousel restaurant on Fifth Avenue, when I would fill him in on the London gossip. I think it was all a bit remote for him: he had been transformed from being a carefree bachelor into a domestic animal, and although he loved the home life he had with his wife and children he still liked to know what was going on.

By 1970 Mark and I were technically separated but still great friends. We were invited that year to spend a weekend with our friends the Cushings, in Newport, Rhode Island. As I was already in New York at the time, I accepted with great pleasure. Newport, however, is the kind of place I dislike: there didn't seem to be any sense of privacy – everyone seemed to know what everyone else was up to all the time. I found it over-wrought, a hotbed of gossip, far too social and un-relaxing – and in fact, I have never been back there since. There was one Newport story related to me by Claus, though, that amused me, about a memorable encounter between Newport society's prime hostess, Mrs John Slocum, and Prince Johannes Thurn und Taxis, head of the princely German house of that name. Prince Johannes found himself seated next to Mrs Slocum at a dinner, and while conversing with her in a perfect *'Allo, 'Allo* German accent and obsequiously clicking his heels, he addressed her as Mrs Scrotum.

Claus and Sunny spent most of their weekends and holidays in their stunning Newport house overlooking the water. A few years into their marriage Sunny had become very reclusive, shunning most of the social life, so while on our visit to the Cushings Mark and I were not surprised to be asked to tea by Claus, rather than dinner, which would have involved inviting most of the locals, the last thing Sunny would have wanted. The setting was idyllic; we sat on the terrace looking out over the Atlantic Ocean and surrounded, to my great pleasure, by a quartet of playful yellow Labradors. Ever the perfectionist, Claus had laid on the most delicious spread: accompanying the perfectly buttered toast was a choice of home-made raspberry jam or the very best pale-grey Beluga caviar – the first and only time I have been offered caviar at teatime.

While I nervously helped myself to the caviar, using a teaspoon so as not to appear too greedy and making sure not a single grain escaped, Mark, never one to hold back, quietly helped himself to two spoonfuls of the stuff, which he heaped on to his plate while chatting politely to Sunny. Toby, the largest of the Labradors, sensing a dog lover in Mark, sat very close to him with his head on his knee, hoping for a titbit. As Mark turned his head towards Sunny, Toby seized the opportunity, promptly buried his snout in Mark's plate and devoured the lot. We all burst out laughing and later, when all the sadness between Sunny and Claus had set in, I recalled how precious the sound of our merriment was, ringing out around that table.

Sometime in the late 1970s on a visit to New York, I noticed during one of our lunches that Claus seemed rather depressed. I knew that he truly loved Sunny and that marriage had been an important and life-changing event for him, but there was evidently something troubling him. Although he was far too loyal to speak a word of criticism against her, I think he felt she had in some way rejected him, withdrawn from him while at the same time seeming to need the security of having him around and close to her. When in 1980 Sunny was discovered in an irreversible coma and Claus was accused of her attempted murder, my entire family were flabbergasted; horrified that anyone could even imagine that he could do such a thing. Knowing Claus as well as we did and knowing too how much he loved her, we knew it was unthinkable that he would ever harm Sunny. Unfortunately, he often made a somewhat sinister impression on people, which did little to improve his image during the trial. There were abundant rumours flying around, including the allegation that he practised necrophilia, an apocryphal story that had begun, ironically, with one of Claus's own rather tasteless jokes against himself and had been picked up and embellished by John Aspinall. We all offered to help Claus by supplying character testimonials, and although he was initially found guilty, he was rightly acquitted after his second trial. During the court case Professor Vincent Marks, Britain's leading expert, was one of a battery of famous professors from the medical faculties of American universities who successfully testified to Claus's innocence at his second trial. Vincent Marks in his recent book *Insulin Murders* (Royal Society of Medicine 2007) expresses his disgust with the few journalists who obstinately continued to prefer a scenario of 'lust and loot' to hard scientific facts.

There were two trials, the second of which was

televised, and at the time I was in Barbados with my brother Alastair's wife, Nico. We knew he was innocent, but all the same it was a marvellous moment when we watched the not-guilty verdict being broadcast to the world; we literally danced around the room, elated that Claus had been vindicated. Of course, life has never again been the same for him, and shortly after his acquittal he moved back to London to be with his beloved daughter Cosima and his friends. Mark gave a welcoming party for him soon after he returned, and it felt so comforting to know that he was in a place surrounded by his friends, all of us so relieved that he had survived this horrific ordeal. Over the years, I had spent enough time with Claus and Sunny to know how much he loved her, and how much in love they had been, and this catastrophic turn of events was distressing and deeply shocking. From time to time I would notice how sad his face looked in repose. It was with great sorrow, but also an inevitable sense of relief, that we learned of Sunny's recent death, releasing her from the coma she had been in for twenty-eight years.

Nowadays Claus lives in London, close to Cosima. He lovingly carries out his grandfatherly duties towards Cosima's three children, proudly boasting about them to all his friends. Until recently he was the music and theatre critic for the *Catholic Herald* and regularly sent me the pieces he wrote, always accompanied by little personal notes, beautifully written and very witty, which never failed to make me laugh. In recent months he has been plagued by ill health but is showing good signs of recovery. We speak several times a week on the phone, and every few months, when he is able to drag me out of my nest, we have supper together at Carluccio's in Richmond and then go on to a play at the Richmond Theatre. Being with him conjures up many good times, and a fragment of my past. I enjoy his company immensely and we still talk as we always have done, through the years and across the continents.

Patrick Plunket, smiling, sitting on the wall in the garden at Pelham Cottage ...

... and contemplating life in the garden at The Mount.

Geoffrey Keating in his uniform. He was an outstanding war photographer and was taken prisoner in 1943 at Anzio during the German occupation.

Geoffrey and his daughter Rima in the garden at Pelham Cottage – Geoffrey was one of our most frequent visitors and often just dropped in to chat and spend time with us.

Above: Claus von Bülow in his legal attire. He practised as a barrister in Lord Hailsham's legal chambers in the 1940s and 50s.

Above right: Sunny von Bülow with Cosima. Sunny was a stunning beauty and radiated a stylish elegance.

Right: Claus on his return to London, with his beloved daughter Cosima.

Tony Lambton in Tuscany,
with his many dogs.

Tony wearing his characteristic sunglasses and a rather
battered straw hat, relaxing
in the sunshine in the
garden at Pelham Cottage.

David Frost and the Shah of Persia. David conducted the last interview with the Shah in Contadora, Panama, shortly before the Shah's death in exile in 1980.

David, Carina and their three sons, Miles, Wilfred and George – best friends to this day with my boys.

David and Carina at a party at Ormeley Lodge.

Rupert, Mark and me having fun on the lawn at
Pelham Cottage, with Noodle.

India Jane and me in the bow
window of Pelham Cottage – this
photograph was taken for *Vogue* and
remains one of my favourites.

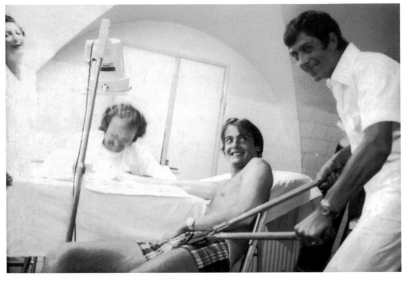

Above: Rupert having his hand stitched by a doctor in Italy whilst on holiday; fortunately the doctor on his left was not in charge of the procedure!

Below: Rupert during a respite while skiing in St Anton

One of my favourite photos of Rupert. I keep it in a simple frame by my bed.

CHAPTER TEN

TONY LAMBTON

Tony Lambton was one of the most magnetic people I have ever met. Famous as a passionate and dedicated lover of women, as well as for his tendency, both political and personal, to push actions and views to controversial levels, he was also a man of high intellect, extremely funny, well read and intensely loyal to his friends.

About 1947 when I was thirteen, my life was considerably brightened when the sophisticated and alluring twenty-five-year-old Tony Lambton strolled into my innocent and protected world. Tall, slim – strikingly Byronic – he wore a bottle-green velvet coat, a decades-early Sergeant Pepper look, way ahead of even a hint of the arrival of hippy clothes for men. In that sea of convention and plain tweeds worn by all the other men around me, he was a figure of glamour and difference. Suddenly, life at Wynyard was suffused with the excitement of my first big crush.

As a child Wynyard was my favourite place to be –
I loved the promise of the three ballrooms, the breath-
less stillness of the chapel and the glorious domed hall,
full of statues. It was, quite simply, a wondrous place
for a child to live. Without the distraction of television,
my brother and sister and I found our own ways of
amusing ourselves. There were over four thousand
acres to roam in and the vastness of the house made it
an ideal place for playing sardines or hide-and-seek.
I discovered the joys of Wynyard's extensive library and
at an early age became an avid reader. My imagination
would soar in that library. I used to imagine that our
pheasants really did fly higher than anywhere else –
this was a local myth deriving from the Londonderrys'
estate having one of the best pheasant shoots in the
country.

We were, however, fairly isolated up there as there
were not many neighbours, and for most of the time
the three of us relied on each other for companionship
and games. We rarely had a friend to stay because when
I was only eleven my mother developed cancer of the
mouth, the horrible disease disfiguring her beautiful
face, and understandably she became very reclusive and
hated being seen. But although guests were therefore
somewhat discouraged, there were some exceptions,
and one person who was allowed to visit was Tony
Lambton whom our parents, being friends of his

parents Lord and Lady Durham, had known since he was a boy. Tony was always happy to visit because not only was he very fond of my mother and father but he also loved Wynyard and the shooting parties. We absolutely loved it when he came over, and Jane, Alastair and I were mesmerised by him. We followed him around, laughing at everything he said because he was so funny, and he instantly became my childhood hero. A flattering comment from him would be mulled over for days; even now I recall him telling me that I had beautiful hands, and the intensity I read into this could occupy me for hours.

Jane and I would vie for Tony's attention. And there was one way in which I thought I could guarantee to captivate him – by putting on a glittering performance, each better than the year before, in our home-directed drama productions. Every Christmas Jane, Alastair and I would put on a play in one of the ballrooms where, during the war, when Wynyard had been a temporary teaching college, a stage complete with theatrical curtains had been built. All the busy tenants on the estate were invited to come and watch (although 'encouraged' might be a more accurate word – they were often rather reluctant). I would choose the subject of the play and write the script. Mrs Worsley, the vicar's wife, would be our producer, and the dressing-up clothes and the idea of being real-life actors and actresses would wildly excite us. Mummy would hire costumes from Nathan's, the theatrical costumiers, and they would arrive with their matching wigs in big boxes sent from London, which would be unpacked and whipped straight into the oven to kill off the crabs which my mother was convinced were seething within the folds. Before the performance, a lot of rehearsing and even more giggling would take place, repeatedly suppressed by the terrifying, squint-eyed Mrs Worsley.

After the triumphant show, and when the estate workers had gone home in silent relief that a whole year would have to elapse before they would be forced to watch another play, Tony would stay for dinner and tell us how wonderful we were and how well we had acted. I would store up his words; listen to the sound of his voice so as to recapture it later. Actually, as he once admitted to me many years later, he was sizing up the two Vane-Tempest sisters. If only I had known!

Tony was definitely a grown-up in my young eyes. He had *experienced* life. Having served in the Hampshire Regiment in the Second World War, he had been invalided out with eye trouble, something that was to become a permanent bother to him, and then had worked as a machinist in a munitions factory in Wallsend, the North Tyneside industrial district. By the age of twenty-three he had already shown his political ambitions by contesting for the Conservatives the

seat of Chester-Le-Street in County Durham in the
election at the end of the war, then in 1950 that of
Bishop Auckland, before finally being elected as a
Member of Parliament in 1951 for Berwick-on-Tweed.
When we first met he was busy serving on the Durham
County Council.

This all added to his glamour.

Tony was already married when he used to come
and visit us, and he had a little daughter, Lucinda.
However, I remember him bringing his family with
him only once on his frequent visits to Wynyard. His
wife Bindy was rather magnificent-looking: tall,
slightly long-faced and horsey-looking, with a tiny
waist, and beautiful in an imposing way. They had
married when he was only twenty-one and she was
twenty, and although they remained married for life,
Bindy continuing to host his shooting and weekend
parties, they each led their own lives. Lucinda impressed me too: although only five or six, she seemed
to have inherited Tony's rapier wit. Tony went on to
have five more children, all of whom adored him.

Tony's temper was volatile, to say the least, and
although we were thoroughly accustomed to our
father's unpredictable behaviour, we had never encoun-
tered anything like Tony in one of his furies. He would
be out shooting, his loader standing next to him, and
if several unexpected birds happened to fly over he

would shout at the flustered man, 'Quickly now!' Occasionally, the loader would be slow in handing him the gun, resulting in Tony missing a bird even though he was a very good shot. At this he would throw himself on to the ground like a child, flinging his gun from his hand in a tantrum of rage, and shout at the grass, the loader, the pheasants and most of all at himself. Later, he would come back to Wynyard for tea, ashamed of himself. My mother would give him a good talking-to, which we thought was hilarious.

As a child I used to think of Tony as the first truly eccentric person I had ever met, but on reflection I have adjusted that thought; with a family like mine, it now occurs to me, perhaps I had never really met anyone who was anything else. Photographs of Tony in his later life almost always show him wearing slightly sinister dark glasses, but even during the dark afternoons of the North of England winter he was already trying them on from time to time, testing out a look to see how far he might go or, more likely, because of his persistent eye problem, protecting his eyes at the same time.

All his life he remained a tremendous lady-killer, and after I was married he admitted to me that he would watch Jane and me and wonder which of us he would pursue when we had reached a suitable age; in the end, when Jane was older he fell passionately in love with her and their affair lasted many years. She definitely had the edge over me, being much the prettier, against my youth and gaucheness, and they also shared a love of shooting.

Tony was incredibly kind to me and when, at nineteen, I was engaged to Mark I experienced at first hand his unflinching loyalty and generosity to those he loved. I was deeply in love with Mark and desperately wanted to marry him, but Daddy was doing his best to forbid the marriage on the grounds that Mark was unsuitable. I no longer had my mother for support, and although Jane and Alastair were on my side I needed the approval of those with more authority. Tony was full of support and encouragement, and gave me two hundred pounds for our honeymoon. This was an enormous sum of money in those days and Mark lost no time in booking the most expensive suite in the Hôtel Lotti, not only the best hotel in Paris but one that was perilously close to Le Circle, a gambling club (Mark of course was an inveterate gambler). Nearly two years later, my twenty-first birthday was largely overlooked by most of my friends and family, as not only was I already married but I also had the key to my own front door and a child and a pram to push through it. Tony and I shared a deep love of Rudyard Kipling, from whom he could quote lengthy passages. Recognising the importance to me of my official coming-of-age, he gave me the

Bombay edition of all Kipling's works, which remains one of my most treasured possessions. I return to it again and again, always finding new insights I have somehow missed during what must be hundreds of readings.

I always tried to return the support and comfort of friendship whenever he needed it. Tony would turn up unannounced at Pelham Cottage, just like everyone else did, coming cheerfully through the garden door to see who else was sitting in the garden. Sometimes he just called in to make me laugh, though later, when scandal threatened to put an end to his parliamentary career, he would arrive in a miserable state, seemingly overwhelmed by adversity and just wanting to talk.

Tony and I shared a passion for dogs and he introduced me to another lifelong love – dachshunds. His own dog, Fly, was the inspiration for Jane's wedding present of Noodle to Mark and me. Tony was enchanted by the later addition to our dog family, Midge, the dachshund puppy Mark had rescued from a French nightclub, and in the early 1960s decided it was time for a marriage between Fly and her. This solemn event was to take place in Pelham Cottage, but our first attempt at getting them together was a complete failure, so we had to get in a breeder who was adept at arranging such couplings and who swore she had never failed in her task. When this very unprepossessing woman arrived, weighing at least twenty stone and with a full cavalry moustache, Tony and I had to leave the room, we were laughing so much – followed hotly by Fly and Midge, who appeared to be terrified of the 'wedding planner'.

'Now this simply will not do,' she said. 'I never have the owners around when these events take place', and taking Midge under one arm and Fly under the other she placed them on a priceless Queen Anne table of Mark's. Tony and I were dispatched to the next room, where we remained doubled up with laughter, listening to the goings-on on the other side of the wall. Finally we were summoned back, and the lady pronounced that the mating had been successful; however, Fly was so furious when Tony picked him up that he uncharacteristically bit him on the tip of his nose. The result was an unfortunate dark-coloured overhang that prompted Tony's rather embarrassed butler to tactfully enquire on and off for the rest of the week as to whether his lordship would like to use a handkerchief.

Tony inspired in me a huge love of literature, and I owe my devotion to some very special books to his recommendation. He was always suggesting books I should read, and amongst these were A. P. Herbert's novel *The Water Gypsies*, written in 1930, and *Gone to Earth* by Mary Webb, an entrancing story ostensibly about a fox cub but in fact with many layers of meaning.

Tony was also a gifted writer and published several books, among them two collections of short stories: *Snow*, which included an imaginary account of the Russians causing an abnormal snowfall throughout Britain, and *Pig*, in essence a study of the German character, in particular their treatment of the Jews. Both were well reviewed, and if he had continued to write fiction he might well have had another successful career. He was a talented letter writer too, and in the letters he sent me, many of which I still have, his descriptions of people he met or knew still make me smile.

Knowing Tony as well as I did, and knowing his low boredom threshold, I can imagine how terrifying it must have been to sit next to him if you did not know him, especially if you were a woman and rather plain. He could exhibit a cruel sense of humour, always wickedly funny, and could be a vindictive, vituperative and most unwelcome enemy. Like an elephant, he never forgot, and could cut anyone down to size, man or woman. He once described Harold Wilson in a published pamphlet as 'a cold calculating man with an ice-cold brain, whose judgement is never disturbed by human relations or human loyalties or anything silly like that'. Tony also quarrelled publicly with another Prime Minister, Harold Macmillan, and being a fairly good mimic he used to regale me with imitations of him which never failed to amuse me (although I never found Macmillan anything but charming).

A certain generation will remember Tony Lambton in his heyday as the arch-lover, the Casanova of his time. Any beautiful woman in London could be certain that Tony would make his attraction to her quite evident; he could charm anyone. From time to time I would look on in fascination at the seduction tactics he would use. He would sit next to his target, find some introductory way to flatter her and, within a heartbeat, transfix her with his hypnotic gaze and alluring talk.

Later, in 1973, the scandal of his personal life and the photographic evidence of the husband of Mrs Norma Levy, one of the prostitutes he was alleged to have frequented, unfortunately eclipsed his parliamentary activities. (His strong principles had resulted in his resignation as Parliamentary Private Secretary to the Foreign Secretary Selwyn Lloyd over his disagreement with the government's decision to take control of the Suez Canal.) When the photographs of him appeared in the newspaper, I was distressed for him and felt dreadfully sorry for Bindy, his children and Claire Ward, who had been his close companion for many years. I was appalled at the way he had been set up. I called him the minute I saw the article; he came round to Pelham Cottage that morning and we sat in the garden talking, his future seemingly shattered, and I tried my best to make him see a clear way ahead.

But it was no good. Feeling betrayed and unable to face life in England any longer, Tony moved to Italy, and for the last thirty or so years of his life he found peace and happiness with Claire at Cetinale, the sensationally lovely seventeenth-century villa near Siena that they shared and where together they restored the magnificent ornamental garden. All their friends visited them there, and Cetinale became a place where people came to talk and learn – Tony was extremely knowledgeable about historic Italian buildings, especially churches – and above all to laugh.

Sometime in November 2006 Claire rang Jane and me to tell us that Tony was not very well and that she felt we should come out and see him. We had met that summer on his annual trip to London, but nonetheless made plans to visit him in the New Year. Sadly, though, in early December he had a massive stroke, and while initially we thought he would make it beyond the holidays, it is to my deepest sorrow and regret that Tony died just days after, and I was not able to reach him in time. If I had, I would have simply and quietly thanked him for our long and infinitely treasured friendship and for the opportunity to have been there for him in his time of need. The fact that Tony and I were lifelong friends was always a great thrill to me.

When my son Rupert tragically went missing in 1986, Tony sent me a copy of Kipling's poem 'My Boy Jack', about the disappearance and death of Kipling's own son. It was a great source of comfort to me and I often still read it; when I do, I think of Rupert and I think of the friendship I shared with Tony.

'Have you news of my boy Jack?'
Not this tide.
'When d'you think that he'll come back?'
Not with this wind blowing, and this tide.

'Has anyone else had word of him?'
Not this tide.
For what is sunk will hardly swim,
Not with this wind blowing, and this tide.

'Oh, dear, what comfort can I find?'
None this tide,
Nor any tide,
Except he did not shame his kind –
Not even with that wind blowing, and that tide.

Then hold your head up all the more,
This tide,
And every tide;
Because he was the son you bore,
And gave to that wind blowing and that tide!

CHAPTER ELEVEN

Cその

DAVID FROST

After we moved into Pelham Cottage – before all the interior renovations began, before the opening of Annabel's – there was a rather blissful period when Mark and I would spend calm evenings together after the children were in bed, enjoying nothing more than a quiet supper in front of the television. Little did we know in those early days that one of our TV heroes, David Frost, would soon become a lifelong friend.

Like many people in the early 1960s, we had discovered the wickedly satirical BBC programme *That Was The Week That Was*, fondly referred to as *TW3*, which we loved for its unprecedented sending-up of the Establishment. Presented by David Frost and starring a highly talented cast including Millicent Martin, Timothy Birdsall, Lance Percival, Bernard Levin, Roy Kinnear and Willie Rushton, *TW3* was brilliantly biting and funny, and we became addicted. As it wasn't possible in those days to record a TV show, *TW3* nights became sacrosanct and, no matter what, Mark and I never went out when it was on. The show was filmed live, and regularly overran its scheduled time. To limit this, the BBC took to showing reruns of *The Third Man* TV series afterwards, but after *TW3* David used to read a synopsis of the episode and the BBC soon had to drop the repeats and allow the show to run over. When Kennedy died, David presented a marvellously measured and informative programme the following day, without a hint of satire, which was shown in the US to much critical acclaim.

After *TW3* ended its run in 1963, David went on to have a dazzling career. He appeared in a succession of programmes with 'Frost' in the title, including in 1966–7 the highly regarded *Frost Report* which he introduced with the legendary Frost signature phrase, 'Hello, good evening and welcome'. He also hosted programmes such as *Through the Keyhole*, and later on, my all-time favourite after *TW3* was *Breakfast with Frost*, which became a must on Sunday mornings.

David was known for pushing the boundaries and I admired him for his willingness to embrace difficult issues. One of the most riveting early interviews he did was with Dr Emil Savundra of the Fire Auto & Marine Insurance Company (FAM), who had at the time allegedly swindled their policy-holders of millions of pounds. Owing to corrupt methods of investment on the part of Savundra, FAM was broke and all claims were left unpaid. During the interview, while Savundra did not deny having received substantial loans, he said that he did not have the money now to pay out to the policy-holders. Calling the members of the audience 'peasants', he gestured towards the widows and widowers of former policy-holders in the front two rows who had been defrauded by him and said: 'I have no legal responsibility for these people and I have no moral responsibility either.' This enraged David, who replied: 'You may have no legal responsibility – though I hope that you do – but how do you get rid of moral responsibility? We'd all like to know that.' The atmosphere was electric, and when the signature tune played as the titles rolled, David strode off the set leaving Savundra sitting there alone. David explained to me later: 'I did not want to stay chatting amiably to the guest, even in silhouette, as if I was no longer angry. Because I was *still* angry.' A week later Dr Savundra was arrested.

I first met David with Jimmy. The two had become friends – they had developed a wonderfully symbiotic relationship, hugely enjoying each other's company – and sometime towards the end of 1964 he took me to have dinner at David's house in Egerton Crescent in Chelsea. David always had interesting guests at his table; many years later I met Elton John and his then wife Renate – and just like Jimmy he would leap up and down from the table during the course of the meal, unable to contain his boundless energy. As I got to know him, I was staggered at David's get-up-and-go. During the 1970s he flew across the Atlantic two or three times a week without showing any sign of tiredness and I used to wonder how on earth he did it. Even now, on holiday, I am staggered by his ability to keep up with all the sports and activities our boys undertake.

Jimmy and I began to see even more of David after he married Lady Carina Fitzalan-Howard, the beautiful daughter of the Duke and Duchess of Norfolk. His marriage was the best thing that ever happened to him – David and Carina remain to this day a most compatible and loving couple – and gave him a settled and happy domestic life. He mellowed and softened in her company and became a most devoted and involved father to their three sons, Miles, Wilfred and George.

Before they married I invited Carina to Ormeley, and she has never forgotten the drama of that Sunday. All my six children were there, and Carina, although too well mannered to comment, was clearly surprised at the speed with which lunch was devoured. My whole family has always eaten much too fast, but none of us were ever a match for Jimmy, whose habit was to retire to the study for coffee when most of his guests were still enjoying their main course. On this particular

Sunday, having wolfed down lunch, David and Jimmy retired with the rest of his group to the study and Carina and I went upstairs. Admiring the garden from my bedroom window, she said suddenly, 'Annabel, do you realise there are two horses careering round your lawn?' and I instantly knew, to my horror, that they must have escaped from the stable. Followed by Rupert, Carina flew into the garden, and the next thing I knew she and Rupert had caught the horses and put them back in the stable. My knee was in plaster at the time and I hobbled down to thank her for her skill in handling the two animals; it wasn't the first time they had escaped and I knew how difficult it was to coax them back. I imagined Carina must be something of an accomplished horsewoman and was amazed when she admitted that she had never had anything to do with horses in her life. I was awed by the dexterity she had shown, and it was then that our deep friendship began.

In the late 1980s Carina, David and their rapidly expanding family became fixtures on all our holidays. We would spend Easter together in Mexico, then join up for part of August in Spain at Torre de Tramores, the beautiful old farmhouse that Jimmy and I bought in 1986. This continues even now – indeed, the idea of August in Spain without the Frosts is unthinkable. Having David and his family to stay is still one of the great pleasures of the summer. The boys are now grown up and are close friends with my son Ben. Unlike their reluctant father – Jimmy could never persuade David to gamble – the boys, taught by Ben, enjoy the odd flutter, and the noise of the dice rattling on the back-gammon board and the dashing up and down the stairs to catch the racing on Channel Four, accompanied by the odd crash as David knocks over another vase, are the defining sounds of our holidays.

I am astonished at David's tolerance of extreme heat: despite the sweltering Spanish temperatures, he has always been a steadfast player on the tennis court. When the sun began to drop a little he and Jimmy would head towards the tennis court. Several sets later David would still be swinging away, not with the kind of grace one associates with Roger Federer but with a determination to return the ball, which he invariably did; he is one of those maddening players who never fail to hit the ball back, even retrieving the drop shots. I used to laugh as Jimmy would retaliate by trying to fire a harder shot at him, but this too would almost always be returned. After two hours, by 9.30 in the cooling evening air, they would be exhausted and come back to the house for a relaxing drink and supper.

Tennis games were not confined to Spain; one of Jimmy's best friends, the financier Jim Slater, had become passionate about tennis, and Jim, David,

Jimmy and his business partner and friend Selim Zilkha would often gather for a game, either at Ormeley or at Jim's home in Esher. The game was taken extremely seriously, particularly as it involved gambling, although I have forgotten whether the bets were laid on the games or the sets or even the shots. But, since David was no gambler, he was quite unfamiliar with the jargon: 'beavering', for example, the term for raising or lowering your bets, was Double Dutch to him. Once, as he stood on the back line expertly returning every ball but not understanding a word they were saying, Jimmy, up at the net, called back to him: 'Tell you what, David – I'll do the negotiating and you do the running.' The same three players tried to teach David backgammon to get him into the gambling way of thinking, but he managed to resist their entreaties.

In fact, David has always been an all-round sportsman, having played not only tennis but also cricket and, of course, football. Before he went to university he was offered a contract with Nottingham Forest Football Club, something that always impressed the children. Over the last two years both Zac and Benjamin have taken up cricket with a vengeance, inspired by my grandsons Sulaiman's and Kasim's talent for the game and encouraged by Jemima. Even Imran has become enthused by his young sons' talent, having rather lost his own interest in cricket since going into politics in Pakistan. After an initial reluctance, Imran is now willing to join matches arranged by Ben, mainly on Ham Common or in my garden. And in the searing Spanish heat the passion for the game goes on. Every afternoon the players, including David and his boys, troop down to the lawn where the stumps are set up and the women and children are all invited to sit around and applaud.

David is one of the kindest people I have ever met. His loyalty and empathetic intuition are second to none and it is an absolute pleasure and privilege to be his friend. I don't think there is anyone else I know who is quite so riveting to talk to – he is, of course, full of endlessly fascinating stories and opinions, his repartee is razor-sharp, and he can be extremely funny. Years ago when he was staying at Tramores, on the way back from a day trip to the old town of Ronda we decided to take a short cut home over the land owned by the businessman Adnan Khashoggi, who at that time was in some kind of financial trouble. When I asked David what the problem was, he replied, 'Well, to cut a long story short, I think it's a case of plenty of Shoggi and no Khash.'

In 1977 Jimmy and I were, by coincidence, in California at the time when David was doing his much lauded interviews with Richard Nixon. Jimmy went to one of the twelve tapings because by then he was more than just a spectator: he was an investor. A few weeks before, David had rung him in the middle of the night as he was still short of $400,000 of the two million that the project cost, and Jimmy had had no hesitation in lending him the money. David had pulled off a real coup in securing these interviews, and looking back, particularly when the full impact of them was felt the world over, it seems quite amazing that after the first day's taping Jimmy and I were sitting calmly dining with David and Caroline Cushing, his girlfriend at the time. I have been asked since if David was aware then that the interviews were leading to Nixon's infamous apology, and while I felt as excited as everyone else that something was unfolding, I can honestly say that I don't think he did. Later, it became clear that David played a key role in this chapter of American history: that first session holds the record for the largest viewing for a political interview – a staggering forty-five million people tuned in. Their legacy lives on in Peter Morgan's critically acclaimed play of 2006, *Frost/Nixon*, and a film of the same name, directed by Ron Howard in 2008, has enabled a whole new generation to become familiar with David's iconic powers as an interviewer.

David was the first person to persuade Jimmy to agree to an in-depth television interview for his series of 1975–6, *We British*, which was broadcast from Manchester. Jimmy was surprisingly nervous, and said to

David before the show, 'Oh God, if I could get out of this, I'd happily pay twenty thousand pounds.' In fact, it was a very successful debut for him, and it was soon after, in 1977, that he pulled off his legendary *tour de force* on the BBC's *Money Programme* hosted by James Bellini and Hugh Stephenson. The two financial journalists attacked Cavenham Limited, his food company, in response to which Jimmy treated the viewers to a mesmeric performance in which he repudiated all their claims by producing the true facts and figures. When Stephenson and Bellini tried to argue back, they could not get a word in edgeways, and Jimmy ended up by ripping off his microphone and walking off the stage. David and he spoke of this virtuoso feat for many years later.

During the twelve years in which *Breakfast with Frost* ran on the BBC, David would interview leading politicians, from prime ministers downwards; it was a serious programme, and compulsive Sunday morning viewing. Everyone wanted to be interviewed by David and appear on his show. When I wrote my autobiography *Annabel: An Unconventional Life* in 2004, I jokingly said to Carina, 'I wish I could go on David's programme and get a few people to buy the book', never dreaming for one moment that I would be able to do so. To my amazement, he asked me on — it was an act of pure loyalty and friendship because he couldn't possibly have really wanted me. The publicist from my publisher was clearly impressed that I had fixed this appearance myself.

I shook with terror until I sat down on that much viewed sofa, where David promptly put me at my ease. He began by asking me about Mrs White, who had once ruled my life with a rod of iron. She was David's favourite character in the book, and he particularly loved the part where she caught me out 'carrying on' as she put it, and proceeded to make my life hell for a while. Then David asked about my marriages to Mark and Jimmy. I meant to say that I was really a one-man woman, instead of which, through sheer nervousness, I said, 'I am basically a one-woman man.' David did not seem to notice my gaffe, nor did he flinch when I nearly knocked down a lamp as I got up from the sofa, but when I arrived home the children roared with laughter, pointing out my mistake.

David came to Zac's circumcision at Pelham Cottage in 1975. The actual procedure took place upstairs, out of sight, but it made David feel very squeamish, especially when my sister Jane came down the stairs and said to him matter-of-factly, 'OK, David, it's your turn now – the rabbi is waiting.' However, the experience did not put him off agreeing to become Ben's godfather, joining a rather incongruous group including Marcia Falkender and Evelyn de Rothschild. Over the years

David and Ben have enjoyed a close relationship; Jemima and Zac are also very fond of David.

After all these years, having watched all our children grow from toddlers into young adults, we have become like one family, totally at ease with each other. David still calls me 'the Divine One', which dates back to something that happened years ago on Sandy Lane Beach in Barbados. While David was busy making sand castles for the boys, Carina and I were having a dip in the sea to cool off. As we emerged, David looked up, opened his arms wide and shouted at the top of his voice for everyone on the beach to hear, 'Ah, here comes the Child Bride and the Divine One!' Heads turned in bewilderment, as Carina may have looked every inch the beautiful Child Bride but they could see no sign of the Divine One.

I have always thought that the reason for David's success as an interviewer is his passionate curiosity about what makes people tick. He believes that everyone has something they can teach you, if you only look hard enough for it. As his father used to say, 'Even a stopped clock is right twice a day.'

CHAPTER TWELVE

RUPERT BIRLEY

On Tuesday 17 June 1986 my beloved eldest son Rupert walked down to the beach at Lomé, the capital of the small country of Togo in West Africa. He had been working in the neighbouring landlocked and poverty-racked country of Burkina Faso, setting up a business to establish a terminal for supplying grain to Nigeria. Mark later called Burkina Faso 'a bloody miserable place' – life expectancy is still only about fifty years – and I knew from what he told me during his visits home, from his friends who would visit him regularly and from his letters that Rupert was longing to leave and come home.

That morning he folded his clothes, took off his watch and removed his wallet, placing them all in a neat pile and tipping the beach boy to look after them. The red flag was up, indicating that the sea, always treacherous at the best of times, was unsafe to swim in. At the time, Rupert was walking with the help of a stick as he had not fully recovered from a terrible leg injury that had left him unable to play some of the sports that he loved, including tennis, which he had played with great passion. Swimming remained the only exercise possible for him, and was helping his leg to get better. His irrepressible spirit of daring had always pushed him too far, leaving him hovering too close to the edge of danger. He had damaged his leg the preceding autumn, while doing wheelies on a motorbike to impress some girls. The bike had fallen on top of him and crushed his leg so badly that when he arrived at the Parkside Hospital in Wimbledon parts of the bone below the knee were sticking out.

The following summer, having returned reluctantly to Lomé, he had set off that June morning as fearless of the elements as he had been all his life, ignoring the sign that warned him against the strong tides and against even entering the water. Rupert had always felt himself to be inviolate; he thought he would live for ever, and so did I. But he never came back and his body was never recovered, and my whole world fell to pieces.

Rupert was my first child; he had arrived in August 1955 after a long and rather tortuous labour. I had only been married to Mark for six months when I found out that Rupert was on the way. Living as we were in the tiny one-bedroom flat at the top of my mother-in-law Rhoda's house in St John's Wood, getting pregnant was the last thing I had planned to do; in fact I was so naive that I made no connection with the awful feeling of sickness I was experiencing at breakfast time. It was only when I heard Mrs White's memorable 'I'm afraid you've fallen' that I realised I might be pregnant. At first I was both amazed and dismayed, but soon afterwards I began to feel that it was extremely grown up to be pregnant before the age of twenty-one, and I settled into my pregnancy quite comfortably.

Rupert was born ten days early, and it was a terrifying childbirth; no one had explained to me what was going to happen, and along with most people of my generation I did not really know anything about how you had babies. My ignorance was compounded by having no one to ask; my mother had died four years earlier, and the sight of Mrs White's gloom-laden expression every time the word 'confinement' cropped up was enough to make me change the subject immediately. But from time to time she couldn't help but frighten me, managing to imbue me with the horrors of her own labour, telling me in lurid detail: 'My Joyce, she took three days to appear.' I remember missing my mother more at that stage in my life than ever before.

As I mentioned earlier, the birth took place in a tiny nursing home at 27 Welbeck Street. It had been established after the First World War and had become an eminently fashionable place to have babies; I believe now it is an equally popular cosmetic surgery hospital. As the labour progressed I made enough noise to outroar a full football stadium at the scoring of a home goal. I didn't know I had the capacity to make such sounds. I had been left entirely alone apart from an elderly sister popping in and out telling me to keep quiet, and with hindsight I realise this was pretty harsh and unkind – very different from attitudes to labour these days. Eventually, once I was ready to push, several nurses appeared and tried to hold me down as I writhed about, screaming and yelling and kicking. When Rupert finally appeared he was whisked away, as during the birth I had become genuinely ill and was incapable of looking after him. I recall my bed being winched up from the bottom because of something to do with postnatal shock, and my sister Jane staring in worried horror at me lying in my oddly angled bed. At that stage I simply wished to be reunited with my dachshund Noodle.

That amazing emotion, that feeling of absolute wonderment and disbelief, the flooding in of unconditional love, coupled with a tigerish instinct to protect that would overwhelm me at the births of Jemima, Zac and Ben, took a few days to come with each of my three older children. I think the delayed response was something to do with my own youth and the experience I had just been through; but on the second day when I was a little better, Rupert was put into my arms and at last I took notice of him and saw that he was already beautiful.

However, looking back I see that I certainly took some time adjusting to my new responsibilities; there were moments when the bossy and exasperating Sister Abel, the monthly maternity nurse who accompanied Rupert and me up to Wynyard after the birth, felt herself beginning to despair. During those six weeks Jane would burst into the nursery begging for the new mother to be released so I could go and play tennis with her. And much as I loved Rupert, I wanted to have the freedom to do all the things I had done before having him. Sister Abel must have sometimes wondered whether it was the baby or the mother who was her main charge. Mark was not much better as a parent because although he had always wanted a boy and was secretly intrigued by the idea of being a father, he certainly never wanted more than one child and in those early years was simply bored by babies.

But my own love for Rupert just grew and grew. From those first few months as an enchanting baby he became an adorable little boy; his beauty was such that it was difficult not to stare at him, all blond hair and extraordinary yellow-green, almost tawny, eyes. People even used to stop me in the street to comment on him. And he was clever; I can remember when he was a toddler reading Beatrix Potter to him as he lay in my bed and suddenly realising *he* was reading to *me* while looking at the pictures. At first I thought he was reciting the words by heart, so I reached for another book and handed it to him; he began to read it, pronouncing the words phonetically and carefully, and it struck me for the first time that he had taught himself to read – before he even went to school. At the age of two and a half he was joined by his brother Robin, and from early on they developed an extraordinary lifelong bond.

We moved into Pelham Cottage when Rupert was three, and when I think of that house I think predominantly of him. The memory of Rupert running happily around the garden is something indistinguishable from the memory of Pelham Cottage, and in that way continues to contribute to the great affection I still feel for the place, which is greater than for anywhere else I have lived. It was there in the lovely garden hidden from the sights and sounds of South Kensington's traffic that Rupert's love of animals began to develop. He became the devoted owner of a chipmunk called Chukka, which he had tamed himself from the wild, even though it is notoriously difficult to train the breed. He was a natural with animals, and Chukka became as much a part of the family as the dogs, with his own specially built squirrel cage. Whenever and wherever Rupert went, Chukka would go with him, never leaving his perch on his shoulder, nestling into his neck or down the sleeve of his sweater. When Rupert was older, I noticed that same gentleness and cherishing nature emerge in his behaviour with very young children, including my godson Henry Brocklehurst and his sister Molly, and then with Ben, Rupert's youngest half-brother, twenty-five years his junior, who was mesmerised by him. They all adored the way he would give them his whole attention, play games and read stories while ignoring all the adults around them. That Rupert would have made a wonderful father I have no doubt at all.

Although Rupert was not able to enrol Chukka at his prep school St Aubyn's near Rottingdean, he did take him to Eton for the first term. I suspect that Mr Bull his housemaster may have failed to notice his presence, but I do know that Rupert had the Dame (the name for a matron at Eton) eating out of his hand, and I am sure she never sneaked on him as he managed to keep Chukka there with him for the first year. On the day that someone at Pelham Cottage left the cage door open and Chukka escaped through the trees, never to be seen again, Rupert was heartbroken. I know that it was his fearless ease with animals that protected him on the day of Robin's terrible accident at Howletts.

Even the comforting presence of Chukka had not been enough to diminish Rupert's homesickness at Eton. At St Aubyn's Mr Gervis the headmaster was a man unusually sensitive for his time, allowing both boys to come out for the weekends with me to spend Saturday nights in a hotel in Brighton. I would bring India Jane with me and we would all have lunch at Wheeler's, our favourite restaurant, before spending the afternoon eating ice-creams and riding on the bumper cars on the two piers, just as Jane and I had done with my father when we were schoolgirls at Southover Manor in Lewes. The boys would work themselves into a state of misery when it was time to go back on Sunday night, and a few years later when Rupert was at Eton his unhappiness at our parting had not got any less. I still have bundles of letters that begin 'Darling darling Mum', then 'I really do hate it here. I am trying to like it but I can't', or similar.

I went down as often as possible to see him, collecting him and later Robin and their friends in my Mini Cooper, their long teenage legs hanging out of the windows as we raced back to London; and I would drive down to meet Rupert in Windsor Great Park to try and work out how to make him less unhappy. I began to consider taking him out of Eton, until Jimmy told me that if I did, it would blight his life. Instead, Jimmy took me away to Jamaica for a few weeks in order to reduce the frequent and agonising contact Rupert and I had with each other. The separation did help a little, and I wrote both boys daily letters full of jokes and laughter. Once the holidays arrived, Rupert went back to his normal cheerful self. Because I was so young I found the children such fun, loving spending time with them, especially taking them to the funfair at Battersea Park. And sometimes I behaved disgracefully on holiday with them at Porto Ercole, creeping up the stairs of Geoffrey Keating's flat where we were staying, to take pictures of him having a naked siesta on his bed, or dressing the boys up as nuns to roam around the streets in the ultra-strict Catholic town.

One advantage of Rupert's homesickness during his schooldays was that instead of socialising he had more time for work, and with the help of his inspirational history reacher Tom Weir he won a history exhibition to Oxford where he read History and Russian at Christchurch.

The children always remained top priority, even when I met Jimmy and my personal life became a little complicated. They never thought Jimmy was anything other than a great friend, and they adored him. Their own naivety, that trusting quality of childhood, as well as Mark's impressive discretion when around the children, preserved their innocence. When Jimmy appeared on the scene during our scruffy holidays, life was suddenly transformed into something ritzier and more exciting. I made sure he never stayed the night when the children were at home from school, and the holidays and half-terms remained sacrosanct. When, many years later Jimmy made the decision to go and live in America, I decided to remain in England with the three youngest children, for although the three older Birley children had left home, I did not want to be away from them either.

When Rupert left Oxford, both Mark and Jimmy (despite having a rule that he would never employ a graduate) wanted Rupert to come and work for them. His intelligence and charm, combined with his academic capabilities, made him an immensely attractive potential employee. Fatherhood had not come easily to Mark when the children were young and it was only when Rupert got into Oxford that he realised his elder son's talent; eventually, with much encouragement from me, they became devoted friends. Rupert was interested in making money, and the twin influences of Jimmy and Mark shaped much of his thinking. In Jimmy he benefited from seeing the model of a great financier and entrepreneur in action, and from Mark he inherited a love of the good things in life as well as owing him that great sense of life's absurdities and his appreciation of lovely clothes and shoes.

But Rupert wanted to make his own way in the world and resisted both men's offers. I believe he was probably destined to become a writer; the letters that he sent me over the years, from Eton, Oxford, Vienna and in particular those when he was working on the *International Herald Tribune* in Russia after he left Christchurch in 1972, made me laugh more than any professional satirist has ever done. In between writing features and articles on human rights, a memorandum on the forthcoming Russian Olympics of 1980 and preparing reports on members of the Politburo, Rupert was socialising with ambassadors and Apollo cosmonauts. However, there was 'not much on the girl front, apart from a very correct Uzbek lady and a number of boozy actresses', he wrote to me. His account of the visit of the daughter of a very senior journalist and descriptions of her hitting the flowing Russian vodka river in a big way as well as sleeping with the Brazilian ambassador were unprintably hilarious. One of his funniest letters was sent from Lomé, where even though he was not enjoying himself much he managed to make me laugh.

If you give unconditional love to your children, you will always get it back. I have also discovered that you never stop being a mother; I am still mother to Robin, India Jane, Jemima, Zac and Ben, even though they are fifty-one, forty-eight, thirty-four, thirty-three and twenty-eight. If any of them hurt themselves or get into trouble, I always want to be there. My children have grown into wonderful parents and my greatest joy is being a grandmother. I adore my grandchildren and try to be as much a part of their lives as I can. Their precious lives are my most treasured gift.

But there was something different about my relationship with Rupert. Having been so very close to me as a little boy, as he grew older our relationship became more than just that between a mother and son and more one of very close friends. The generation barrier dissolved, and as he became an adult I was still young enough to go out to dinner with him as an equal. Sometimes I wonder if I have exaggerated in my mind the intensity of our closeness, but I honestly do not think I have ever had such a bond with anyone.

There is something about the startling phenomenon of the firstborn that never goes away. I believe there was nothing Rupert did not share with me; I knew everything about his girlfriends and I would shake with laughter at his accounts of his amatory exploits, usually told against himself. His love affairs were always uproariously chaotic and complicated. The object of one, in Russia, was only able to meet him in a graveyard as her husband was very jealous and prone to following her everywhere she went. There was not a single gravestone upon which Rupert and his Russian lady had not recorded their mutual ardour, each encounter marked by a pattern of mosquito bites across his back. I wished that he and his girlfriend Bettina von Hase, warm, clever, beautiful and adorable, had met when they were a little older – she would have been a perfect daughter-in-law.

When Mark came to see me at Ormeley a week after my birthday in June 1986 and told me that Rupert had gone missing overnight, I could barely believe what I was hearing; in a state of total terror, I begged him to tell me it was not true. So long after Rupert's still unexplained death, the lack of finality continues even today to lurk in the back of my mind. Logic tells me that, having gone down to one of the most treacherous beaches in the area, where it was imperative not to go into the sea when the red flag was up warning that a current could take him out but not bring him back in again, he ignored the warning and was caught by the relentless power of the tide, swept out to sea for maybe hundreds of miles. But I am only 98 per cent certain that is what happened; because his body was never found, there is always that tiny, tiny doubt. Was he picked up by the Russian boat moored in the harbour at the time? Was there any truth, given his fluency in Russian, in the rumours that he might have been working as a spy? I can never be completely sure.

In the few weeks after Rupert disappeared, I waited every evening by the telephone for some news from Mark, who had flown straight out to Lomé with Robin, where they hired a private investigator. Mark would not let me go with them, even though I longed to, as he thought it would be too painful for me, but he confided afterwards how he came to dread the daily call he would have to make to tell me that the detective had found nothing; later on, I found it hard to talk to Mark about Rupert. I received hundreds of letters from people who had known and adored my exceptional son, many of them referring to him as 'an almost perfect human being'. Three months after Rupert's disappearance we held a memorial service at St James's, Piccadilly. I was told the church was packed and that there was an impressive number of beautiful young women there, deeply and audibly distressed, but I remember very little of the occasion.

There is no resting place for Rupert, there is no grave; I planted a copper beech tree in the garden that reminds me of him. I have of course all his letters in which I can still hear his voice full of laughter and love, and I have photographs of him all over the place at Ormeley so I can look at him the whole time. I derive much comfort from simply holding his watch and his wallet that were brought back to me from the beach where he had left them on the morning he went for that last fateful swim, but he is not here, and I miss him every single day.

Rupert was a wonderful letter writer, as I have said, and I have bundles of them from all stages of his life. They are his legacy to me and I often sit reading them, hearing his voice and imagining him still here. I have chosen this one from Africa to end these reflections, because it sums up his sense of humour and his marvellous powers of observation:

Lomé

1 July 1984

Darling Mum,

Just a short note to let you know that I am installed in a huge suite in Hotel 2 Février (so named because the President's Plane crashed on the 2nd February 1974 and he survived) which is decorated in mauve plush and which is full of gadgetry, none of which works.

I'm beginning to get the hang of life in Africa: you need *incredible* patience and the ability to laugh at anything – whatever happens. The first evening in the hotel restaurant the waitress picked up a plate under from which scuttled three huge cockroaches. Far from looking abashed she screamed with laughter and then called the head waiter who burst into giggles as well.

I was invited to a typical African lunch yesterday and have not looked at food since. I was invited for 1 o'clock and duly arrived on time. No food whatsoever and a gaggle of Africans all talking animatedly in a mixture of French and dialect. First drinks: a butler wearing a very tattered smock whose legs were covered in huge scabs appeared with a tray of something called Pom Pom which is dark green, fizzy and so revolting I was almost sick on the spot. Then on with the video: a 1960s French soft-porn number called 'Passion' with no sound except a low crackling noise whose plot consisted of long conversations (inaudible) between a very fat blonde with huge knockers and a very slimy looking Georgie Best look alike. Every 15 minutes exactly there would be the same scene of his white bottom bobbing up and down and of her face showing an expression of ecstasy. At this stage the crackling and the hissing from the video would get much louder (presumably music) and there would be roars of approval from the Africans, '*Ah, illes travaillent, quoi,*' and (groan) more Pom Pom would be ordered. This went on until 4.30 by which time our host had generously opened a bottle of a liquor called GBOMA ABRICOT of which I was forced to drink endless glasses.

Finally the food was brought in by a succession of very fat African ladies. The main course was served in what looked like a huge dustbin lid, and as the guest of honour I was given a massive helping. The ingredients consisted of goats' balls in bright orange grease, tripe and cow's skin (still covered in hair) – all washed down with a tumbler of Pom Pom.

I bought one of those huge Japanese Jeeps as the roads here are riddled with potholes the size of bomb craters. I have also hired a very sweet African called Cissé as a driver. Cissé describes himself as a rally driver and wears an apple green bomber jacket and a pair of size 15 Turkish slippers (with curly toes) in white patent plastic (bought specially for the job). He is enormously proud of the car which he polishes feverishly every morning.

Needless to say he has already had a crash. He came to pick me up one morning and I noticed he was unusually subdued. He confessed that he had had a small accident but that the other driver was completely to blame. Unfortunately for Cissé the other driver was a Frenchman who immediately sent a very detailed telex to our insurance company outlining what had happened. As the owner of the car I was summoned with Cissé to give our version of the story. According to Cissé the Frenchman had pulled out to overtake him just at the moment that about 4 cars were coming the other way. To avoid a head on collision with the oncoming traffic, Cissé in true rally driver style had simply pulled across the road thereby demolishing the front of Mr Defou's Mercedes.

'Well, Cissé,' I asked, 'what did happen?'

Cissé looked slightly taken aback by the scowling insurance man and then thought deeply for about ten minutes. Finally his face lit up as he had remembered what had happened. The road was completely empty at the time and he had moved into position to overtake the Mercedes. Just as he was overtaking the stupid Frenchman had accelerated on purpose and smashed into him. This was recorded on the claim form in illiterate French. Cissé could not understand about drawing a sketch of the accident for the form and insisted on producing a profile of the jeep.

There is nothing to do in the evening apart from going to the cinema (Bruce Lee and *Jesus of Nazareth* have been showing for the last two years).

Tennis is quite fun, particularly as the ball boys (of which there seem to be about 60) do everything for one. Because I have been quite generous with tips, they have decided that I should be given hearty vocal support whenever I play. The worse I play the louder the squeals of support become.

'*Bien joué, Rupert,*' 60 little voices chant, as yet another ball goes sailing out of the court. All this to the great annoyance of the extremely professional

French four on the neighbouring court who are completely ignored and who have to shout to make themselves heard above the din. Things are beginning to get out of control as the ball boys have now discovered when I go swimming and have taken to invading the pool swarming like ants over a lot of very well oiled French women to ask me when I am playing.

Will be back at the end of July.

Love

Rupert

ACKNOWLEDGEMENTS

I would like to thank the following. First and foremost my secretary Judith Naish, in particular for once again managing to decipher my handwriting, her perspicacity in spotting my errors and her general patience and kindness.

My brother Alastair Londonderry for his description of his safari with John Aspinall, and Jonathan Aitken for his hilarious description of Geoffrey Keating on his Middle Eastern trip.

I would also like to thank George Weidenfeld, who suggested the concept of the book; also Alan Samson, Gillian Stern, Lucinda McNeile and Helen Ewing for their invaluable help.